Hoover Institution Studies 36

Marx's Theory of Exchange, Alienation and Crisis

Marx's Theory of Exchange, Alienation and Crisis

Paul Craig Roberts
and
Matthew A. Stephenson

Hoover Institution Press
Stanford University
Stanford, California

The Hoover Institution on War, Revolution and Peace, founded at Stanford University in 1919 by the late President Herbert Hoover, is a center for advanced study and research on public and international affairs in the twentieth century. The views expressed in its publications are entirely those of the authors and do not necessarily reflect the views of the staff, officers, or Board of Overseers of the Hoover Institution.

Hoover Institution Studies 36
International Standard Book Number 0-8179-3361-1
Library of Congress Card Number 79-91039

Printed in the United States of America

For J.M.B., R.H.C.,
and G.W.N.

Contents

Preface

This book claims to be an exposition of Marx's economics, no more and no less. Yet many may find here a different perspective. Those who have viewed Marx as a "minor post-Ricardian" [1] and as a precursor of Keynesian macro-dynamics [2] may be surprised by our argument that Marx was an organizational theorist who saw different economic systems as different forms of social organization. The reader may be startled to discover that economists such as Frank Knight, James M. Buchanan, and Kenneth Boulding, who see economics as the study of how people organize themselves by means of exchange, [3] have more in common with Marx than many of those who consider themselves Marxists. Professed Marxists who employ a vocabulary of humanism may be disappointed to find that they are not Marxists at all.

In this book we show that Marx's concepts of property, money, capital, wages, economic crises, and alienation are derived from his concept of the market system as a form of social organization. This clarifies the meaning of Marxian socialism. According to Marx, what principally distinguishes socialism from capitalism is not property forms and income distribution but the way in which people organize themselves in society. Whereas other socialists focus on altering property forms and income distribution, Marx was primarily concerned with making changes in social organization. He wanted to abolish the market as a system of social organization and to eliminate voluntary exchanges by individuals as the basis for relations between men.

The purpose of this book is to show the central role of exchange in Marx's analysis. We base ourselves on Marx's theory as he wrote it, and not as others have interpreted it, and we emphasize aspects of his thought that have been altogether overlooked or insufficiently stressed by other scholars. Our exposition involves us with one topic, alienation, that is cluttered with controversy. Our explanation of Marxian alienation differs from the others and, in our view, resolves the controversy. We show that Marx's concept of alienation is materialistic and compatible with historical materialism. The fact that Marx has a concept of alienation in his work does not imply that his work is humanistic. To the contrary, we show that Marx's world view denies the existence of good will among men as a basis for humane methods of social change, and instead justifies an unbridled violence that is incompatible with humanism.

Oscar J. Hammen, in two fine studies,[4] has argued that alienation does not play a significant role in Marx's work. But the concept of alienation toward which Hammen has directed his critical attention is a different concept from Marx's and belongs to those who interpret Marx as a humanist. We wish to make it clear that Hammen's critique does not apply to our exposition of Marxian alienation. In his helpful review of this book he wrote: "I see clearly what you mean by insisting that Marx clung to the concept of alienation in the later years even if he did not use the term—namely in the same general 'economic' sense in which he applied it in 1844."

Our emphasis on the theoretical aspect of Marx should not be misconstrued to mean that we disagree with those who emphasize the personal factor in Marx. Our purpose is not to subordinate Marx to his theory, but to throw some new light on Marx the theorist. Neither is our purpose to write an encyclopedic critique of Marx's work or to evaluate Marxian debate.

We agree with Thomas Sowell, who points out that in Marx's treatment economic crises are solely the result of disproportionality.[5] From Marx's viewpoint, this means that crises are a consequence of the social organization of capitalism—that is, a consequence of exchange. In an appendix we show the similarity between Marx's analysis of economic crises and some recent analyses of market disequilibrium.

We wish to thank William Breit, John Gurley, Oscar J. Hammen, and Gordon Tullock for reviewing the manuscript.

Stanford, California P.C.R.
Spartanburg, South Carolina M.A.S.

— 1 —

Marx As An Organizational Theorist

Marx approaches economic organization in terms of the purpose of production. He acknowledges two purposes of production: for direct use, and for exchange. Although he studied both organizational types and defined future society in terms of production for direct use, most of his writing is about production for exchange, which is production for sale on the market.

PRODUCTION FOR DIRECT USE

The primary characteristics of production for direct use are organizational. First, men are directly associated; that is, commercial principles do not intervene in the economic relations between men. Second, the products of production take a direct form as use-values for the community; that is, production is not separated from consumption or use by the process of exchange. These characteristics mean that each man's production and consumption is consciously related to the community's production and consumption, and that products do not find their way into use through being bartered or sold in a market.

Marx found production for direct use to be characteristic of pre-capitalist economic systems, and he designated it as characteristic of the post-capitalist economic system—which would be socialism or communism. In the *Grundrisse* * Marx speaks of "Asiatic," "ancient," "feudal," and "Germanic" categories of production for direct use. In *Capital* and other writings, he gives the patriarchal family, the feudal manor, the ancient Indian commune, and the Inca state in Peru as specific examples of economies organized according to production for direct use.

Marx compares the position of an individual in a pre-capitalist economy with his role in the future socialist economy. In a pre-capitalist economy the labor of the individual is viewed as a portion of the labor of the family or community, and it is seen the same way in the future socialist economy. In both pre- and post-capitalist economies, the labor of individual producers is consciously applied as the combined labor of the community. Producers are not mutually independent.

For Marx, man's human function is work. Man realizes himself in labor. In economies organized for production for direct use, the relations between men are convivial rather than commercial, and society has control over the allocation and employment of labor. This follows from producing use-values for direct consumption by the community rather than "commodities" which find their way into consumption indirectly by being sold in a market. When Marx says that the feudal serf

* The *Grundrisse* was not published in Marx's lifetime. A section of it is available in English as *Pre-Capitalist Economic Formations* (New York: International Publishers, 1965). An edited selection is offered by David McLellan (ed.), *The Grundrisse* (New York: Harper and Row, 1971).

and future socialist man have control over their own labor, he means that labor itself, as well as the products of labor, is not a commodity sold in the market, so that man's "life activity" (work) is not subject to control by the impersonal market and the crises that result from its anarchic nature. The social division of labor is not established by market exchange, and the employment of labor is not subject to the anarchy of the market.

When Marx says that men have control over production, he does not mean that they are free in any absolute sense, or that they are not exploited. He states explicitly that "capital has not invented surplus labor," [1] and he was very much aware that the serf owed labor obligations and that the corvée did not permit the peasant to control the conditions of his work or the products of his labor. More generally, Marx was aware of the discipline and appropriation imposed by a hereditary social division of labor which might support a ruling class in relative luxury. When he writes of a society in which men have control over the process of production, in general he refers to a society in which the products of labor and labor itself do not take the form of "commodities" and do not acquire a life independent of man and a power over him.

There is a difference in the sort of control over work that man has in pre- and post-capitalist economies. Although both systems are characterized by social control over production, in pre-capitalist economies the social division of labor may be subject to superstitious tradition and the community subject to the whims of nature. In socialism, man uses science to plan production and consciously shape his own history.

PRODUCTION FOR EXCHANGE

The primary characteristics of production for exchange or sale in a market are also organizational: producers are mutually independent; and exchange separates production from use or consumption. The separation of production from use produces the "commodity" (which has a life independent of man) and the commodity mode of production. From this mode of production follow capital, wage labor, the separation of value from price, economic crises, and alienation. That these are historically unique aspects of a historically unique mode of production is the main theme of Marx's work. His views on topics such as private property, exploitation, and alienation cannot be understood independently of his views concerning the commodity mode of production. Therefore, to understand Marx we must begin with his concept of the commodity mode of production.

— 2 —

The Commodity Mode Of Production

Capital and *A Contribution to the Critique of Political Economy* begin with an analysis of the commodity and the commodity mode of production. From the time Marx first began to study economics, he sought to separate those economic categories and principles that applied to all economic systems from those that were specific to capitalism or were predominant under capitalism. One should not lose sight of this fact, although some who become immersed in the details of Marx's analytical superstructure frequently do. That superstructure is based upon Marx's analysis of commodities and the commodity mode of production, analysis which contains his conclusion that capitalism will pass away as a consequence of its internal contradictions that result from the separation of production from use. Some scholars have lost sight of Marx's analysis of the first principles of capitalism so completely as to assert that there is no such thing in Marx as the commodity mode of production. But Marx says: "The mode of production in which the product takes the form of a commodity, or is produced directly for exchange, is the most general and most embryonic form of bourgeois production." [1]

Marx's ideas about the nature of the commodity mode of production first appear in *The Economic and Philosophic Manuscripts of 1844*. The concept is thoroughly developed in the *Critique of Political Economy* and in *Capital*, and a succinct definition is provided by Engels in *Anti-Dühring:* "What are commodities? Products made in a society of private producers more or less separate from each other, and therefore in the first place private products. These private products, however, become commodities only when they are made, not for use by their producers, but for use by others, that is, for social use; they enter into social use through exchange. The private producers therefore stand in a social relation, constitute a society." [2]

The distinguishing characteristic of a commodity is that it is produced for exchange—or in other words, for the market. The commodity mode of production refers to that form of society in which producers are related to one another through the market and the "cash nexus."

Marx says that a commodity is "a mysterious thing." [3] In a commodity are "the antithesis [between] use-value and [exchange] value; the contradictions that private labor is bound to manifest itself as direct social labor, that a particularized concrete kind of labor has to pass for abstract human labor; the contradiction between the personification of objects and the representation of persons by things." [4] As we shall show in subsequent chapters, crises and alienation are immanent in these contradictions. To understand Marx, then, we must know what these terms mean.

To have value, a thing must embody human labor, and "the magnitude of the value of any article" is determined by "the amount of labor-time socially necessary for its production." [5] To have use-value a thing must have utility. "The utility of a thing makes it a use-value." [6] Marx says that "a thing can be a use-value, without having value" [7] and gives air and natural meadows as examples.

Use-values, then, may be gifts of nature or products of human labor. Marx calls labor that produces use-value "useful labor." [8] Private or individual labor and particularized concrete labor refer to a specific form of labor, such as that of a tailor.

Use-value results from the specific form of a thing—for example, a coat—and a coat has value because it embodies the labor of a tailor and a weaver. Thus, when a coat gives utility, or is consumed as a use-value, it is particular concrete forms of labor, those of a tailor and weaver, that are consumed. By Marx's definition, things such as natural meadows, which are not produced by human labor, have no value (although in a commodity economy they will have exchange value or market price, because they possess use-value).

Use-values may or may not be produced in the form of commodities. If they are, there is also a money form of value called exchange value (market price). If commodities exchange in proportion to the labor embodied in them, then exchange values are proportional to values, and the labor time expended in their production was socially necessary—that is, all the commodities produced possessed use-value or had utility to the society. According to Marx, in a commodity economy there is no way of knowing whether the products of production have utility until they are exchanged. If such products cannot be exchanged (sold), they are not use-values to the society, and the labor expended in their production was wasted. Wasted labor means, in Marx's terms, that private labor failed to become social labor. Whereas use-value and value exist in every society and without regard to the mode of production, exchange value is specific to commodity production.

Marx says that "the exchange values of commodities must be capable of being expressed in terms of something common to them all." [9] This common element is "homogeneous human labor" or "human labor in the abstract." This means that the specific qualities of commodities and the particular concrete forms of the labor embodied in commodities are "put out of sight" [10] in a quantitative money measure. Thus, exchange value, which "is the only form in which the value of commodities can manifest itself or be expressed," [11] "represents human labor in the abstract, the expenditure of human labor in general." [12] Money as a measure of value is a measure of abstract general labor. The specific concrete forms of labor are lost by their abstraction into money. This occurs only in a commodity economy, because only in such an economy does social labor exist as an aggregation of the labors of mutually independent producers. In a tribal, feudal, or socialist society, individuals do not exist as autonomous producing units. Therefore, there is no need for the abstract quantitative expression of the specific forms of socially useful labor.

In a commodity economy, goods enter into social use through exchange and thus must take an abstract (money) form. Goods that cannot be exchanged (sold) cannot serve a social use. In such an economy, private labor or the labor of individuals can become social labor and serve society only by taking an abstract form. In non-commodity economies, goods do not have to pass through exchange and take an abstract form in order to serve as use-values in society. In non-commodity economies, social labor always takes particular concrete forms, and private labor can directly become social labor without having to become abstract general labor.

When Marx speaks of "the personification of objects and the representation of persons by things," he is emphasizing that commodities have a life of their own. They stand outside of man and have a power over him. The products of man's own hand become a blind force that rules him. Exchange values (market prices) "vary continually, independently of the will, foresight, and actions of the producers. To them their own social action takes the form of the action of objects, which rule the producers instead of being ruled by them." [13] "The process of production has the mastery over man, instead of being ruled by him."[14] "Production relations are converted into entities and rendered independent in relation to the agents of production . . . movements of market-prices, periods of credit, industrial and commercial cycles, alternations of prosperity and crises, appear to them as overwhelming natural laws that irresistibly enforce their will over them, and confront them as blind necessity."[15] "As, in religion, man is governed by the products of his own brain, so in capitalist production, he is governed by the products of his own hand."[16]

CAPITALISM

Marx considered capitalism to be the final and most advanced form of commodity production. It arose out of the dissolution of feudal society, a dissolution which produced a growing multitude of free workers who sold labor services in the market. These workers possessed no property rights in the means of production. The only property rights they had were the rights they possessed in their own labor services, which they sold to the capitalist for money in order to buy the means of subsistence. Marx believed that the worker under capitalism is free in a twofold sense. First, he is free from the bonds of serfdom or community and can sell his labor services to whomever he pleases, that is, his labor services are free from claims by a community or lord. Second, he is free from ownership of the means of production. Since the worker possesses no property rights in the means of production, he possesses no property rights in his own output. He sells his labor services, and the product embodying his labor belongs to the capitalist.

According to Marx, the capitalist stage of commodity production can be designated by the symbols M-C-M′, which mean that the capitalist begins with money which he changes into commodities and back into money. M′ is (hopefully) greater than M. Thus, the purpose of capitalist production is to produce goods for sale in order to make a profit. Marx does not equivocate when he says that "Capitalist production is distinguished from the outset by two characteristic features. First, it produces its products as commodities. . . . The second distinctive feature of the capitalist mode of production is the production of surplus-value [profit] as the direct aim and determining motive of production." [17]

The stage of commodity production before capitalism is simple commodity production, designated by C-M-C, which means that a farmer or an artisan produces a commodity which he sells for money in order to purchase items that he needs but does not produce for himself. Markets for goods exist, and merchants may operate in them in order to make a profit, but the purpose of production itself is not money-making but the fulfillment of needs. C-M-C is commodity production, and producers are mutually independent, but labor markets as such do not exist or are not extensive. Under C-M-C the products of labor are commodities, but labor is not generally a commodity. "A merchant could buy every kind of commodity, but labor as a commodity he could not buy." [18] With the appearance of labor markets, the commodity mode of production reaches the capitalist stage: "The whole system of capitalist production is based on the fact that the workman sells his labor power as a commodity." [19] Marx says that "the production and circulation of commodities are the general prerequisites of the capitalist mode of production." [20] How do these prerequisites become established—that is, how does production for sale on the market arise?

The first trade took place between communities that had accumulated surplus products beyond their needs or wants. Marx says: "as I have before remarked, the exchange of products springs up at the points where different families, tribes, communities, come into contact; for, in the beginning of civilization, it is not private individuals but families, tribes, etc., that meet on an independent footing." [21] According to Marx, then, the first exchange took place between communities rather than within communities. But as soon "as products once become commodities in the external relations of a community, they also, by reaction, become so in its internal intercourse."[22] So exchange has a purpose of its own, and "the commodity form and money penetrate the internal economy of the community directly associated for production; they break one tie after another within the community and dissolve the community into a mass of private producers."[23]

In the past, the dissolution of societies by exchange coincided with their decline, and capitalism did not emerge. Historically, the development of exchange that gave birth to capitalism originated in the interstices of feudal society. Markets developed on the periphery and moved into the center, culminating in a labor market formed of peasants who were uprooted from the soil and artisans who were separated from the means of production. Peasants, artisans, and feudal retainers merged into the worker—the seller of labor services for money—all victims of a change in the social division of labor caused by the relentless extension of exchange.

Capitalism, then, is the result of a historical process through which labor services ("labor power" in Marx's terminology) become commodities. The capitalist as the buyer and user of labor services is a historical creation. He is produced by the development of exchange. According to Marx, the seller of labor power and the owner of money meet in the market and enter into mutual relations as commodity owners.[24] The owner of money is the capitalist. The emergence of labor services as commodities implies the emergence of the capitalist. Once the capitalist appears, he requires a ready supply of labor services. The development of exchange produces both capitalist and worker.

LABOR AND LABOR POWER

In *Pre-Capitalist Economic Formations* (which comes from the *Grundrisse*), Marx made a distinction between labor and labor power (labor services or labor time) that he was careful to retain throughout the remainder of his work. When the capitalist purchases labor power, he is purchasing the worker's time or capacity for labor. Labor is defined as the use of labor power or work. Once having bought the worker's time, it is up to the capitalist to extract the actual mental and physical effort, or labor, from the worker.

Paul Sweezy and others emphasize that the distinction between labor and labor power is an important one in Marx's system, but they do not say why. What is missing in interpretations of Marx is the connection between different modes of production and the concepts of labor and labor power.

The expenditure of human labor is not unique to any mode of production. It is not a factor that enables us to distinguish between the commodity mode of production and non-commodity modes of production. Marx stated: "labor is a natural condition of human existence, a condition of material interchange between man and nature, quite independent of the form of society. On the other hand, the labor which posits exchange value is a specific social form of labor." [25]

It is misleading to emphasize the obvious fact that human labor is necessary for the production of commodities. Labor is a necessary condition in every form of society. It is required to produce commodities, but it also produces products that are not commodities, products intended for one's own use or products produced in societies in which there is no exchange. In contrast, labor power is unique to capitalism. It is exchange that distinguishes commodity production from non-commodity modes of production. Labor power is specific to exchange. It is a commodity.

EXCHANGE

In view of the importance our interpretation places on exchange as the principal element in Marx's vision of capitalism, it is necessary to understand what Marx meant by that term.

The key lies in Marx's view of the status of individuals in society. According to Marx, exchange is the cause of persons being mutually independent, rather than directly associated as they are in a family or in a communal society. Exchange is the social interaction of persons that are mutually independent. Exchange begins between mutually independent communities.

Historically, exchange makes independent communities dependent and makes dependent members within communities independent. Between communities a new "social division of labor arises from the exchange between spheres of production that are originally distinct and independent of one another." [26] Within communities "the particular organs of a compact whole grow loose, and break off, principally owing to the exchange of commodities with foreign communities, and then isolate themselves so far that the sole bond, still connecting the various kinds of work, is the exchange of the products as commodities. In the one case, it is the making dependent what was before independent [communities]; in the other case, the making independent what was before dependent [individuals]." [27] Thus exchange destroys communities in both ways. Formerly independent communities are incorporated in a commodity relation which then penetrates the internal economies and dissolves them "into a mass of private producers" producing for market.

There is a contemporary view that sees exchange as a very general form of social system.[28] According to this view, exchange takes place not only between independent individuals in a market but also between members of families, members of various institutions and organizations, and citizens engaging in political activity. For example, informal exchange takes place within families principally as a result of the division of labor between husband and wife. There is no formal bargaining or contracting but each member of the family contributes and in return expects to benefit from the services of other members. Another example is provided by politicians, who in effect exchange promises in return for votes.

Marx's concept of exchange is not as broad. By exchange Marx means *only* market exchange. He does not call other forms of swapping exchange. Neither does he apply the term to the division of labor within a factory, nor to the social division of labor. To understand Marx, it is necessary not to confuse exchange with the division of labor. Marx is unequivocal in explaining that the division of labor in a society can be a product of either hereditary tradition, a central plan, or exchange. It is best to let Marx himself state the difference between division of labor and exchange:

> To all the different varieties of values in use there correspond as many different kinds of useful labor, classified according to the order, genus, species, and variety to which they belong in the social division of labor. This division of labor is a necessary condition for the production of commodities, but it does not follow, conversely, that the production of commodities is a necessary condition for the division of labor. In the primitive Indian community there is social division of labor, without production of commodities. Or, to take an example nearer home, in every factory the labor is divided according to a system, but this division is not brought about by the operatives mutually exchanging their individual products. Only such products can become commodities with regard to each other, as result from different kinds of labor, each kind being carried on independently and for the account of private individuals.[29]
>
> . . .
>
> But, in spite of the numerous analogies and links connecting them, division of labor in the interior of a society, and that in the interior of a workshop, differ not only in degree, but also in kind. The analogy appears most indisputable where there is an invisible bond uniting the various branches of trade. For instance, the cattle-breeder produces hides, the tanner makes the hides into leather, and the shoemaker, the leather into boots. Here the thing produced by each of them is but a step towards the final form, which is the product of all their labors combined. There are, besides, all the various

> industries that supply the cattle-breeder, the tanner, and the shoemaker with the means of production. Now it is quite possible to imagine, with Adam Smith, that the difference between the above social division of labor, and the division in manufacture, is merely subjective, exists merely for the observer, who, in a manufacture, can see with one glance, all the numerous operations being performed on one spot, while in the instance given above, the spreading out of the work over great areas, and the great number of people employed in each branch of labor, obscure the connection. But what is it that forms the bond between the independent labors of the cattle-breeder, the tanner, and the shoemaker? It is the fact that their respective products are commodities. What, on the other hand, characterizes division of labor in manufactures? The fact that the detail laborer produces no commodities. It is only the common product of all the detail laborers that becomes a commodity. Division of labor in society is brought about by the purchase and sale of the products of different branches of industry, while the connection between the detail operations in a workshop is due to the sale of the labor-power of several workmen to one capitalist, who applies it as combined labor power. The division of labor in the workshop implies concentration of the means of production in the hands of one capitalist; the division of labor in society implies their dispersion among many independent producers of commodities. While within the workshop, the iron law of proportionality subjects definite numbers of workmen to definite functions, in the society outside the workshop, chance and caprice have full play in distributing the producers and their means of production among the various branches of industry.[30]

To understand exchange, we should remember that to be a commodity it is not enough for a product to be produced as a useful thing for others. Marx says:

> A thing can be useful and the product of human labor without being a commodity. Whoever directly satisfies his wants with the produce of his own labor, creates, indeed, use-val-

> ues, but not commodities. In order to produce the latter, he must produce not only use-values, but use-values for others, social use-values. (And not only for others, without more. The medieval peasant produced quit-rent corn for his feudal lord and tithe-corn for his parson. But neither the quit-rent corn nor the tithe-corn became commodities by reason of the fact that they had been produced for others. To become a commodity a product must be transferred to another, whom it will serve as a use-value, by means of an exchange).[31]

Engels footnotes this passage: "I am inserting the parenthesis because its omission has often given rise to the misunderstanding that every product that is consumed by someone other than its producer is considered in Marx a commodity."

Marx saw the individualism that became distinctive of nineteenth-century behavior as the product of exchange. He wrote: "But man is only individualized through the process of history. He originally appears as a generic being, a tribal being, a herd animal. . . . Exchange itself is a major agent of this individualization. It makes the herd animal superfluous and dissolves [the herd]." [32]

As pointed out, in order for labor services to become commodities, the worker must be free. The worker is free from the "old relation of clientship, villeinage, or service," [33] and becomes free to contract and exchange. Although Marx was contemptuous of this bourgeois freedom, his view of the social change taking place coincides with that of his contemporary, Sir Henry Maine, who believed that the "movement of progressive societies has hitherto been a movement from status to contract."

The idea that exchange is specific to the commodity mode of production probably came to Marx after he read critically Adam Smith and J. B. Say and after he read Engels' essay "Outlines of a Critique of Political Economy" published in 1844. In what Marx referred to as a "brilliant essay on the critique of economic categories," [34] Engels wrote: "The opposition between the real inherent utility of the thing and the determination of that utility, between the determination of utility and the freedom of those who exchange, cannot be superseded without superseding private property; and once this is superseded, there can no longer be any question of exchange as it exists at present." [35]

Here is the idea, expressed by a young Engels, that exchange will have to be eliminated. Marx was also interested in what Adam Smith and J. B. Say said about exchange, as shown by the extensive notes he made in the 1844 *Manuscripts*. He recognized that Smith regarded the "propensity to truck, barter, and exchange one thing for another" to be a part of human nature and therefore a feature of every society. If one adopted Smith's view, exchange could not be the basis for distinguishing one mode of production from another. It is significant, therefore, that Marx noted that J. B. Say regarded exchange "as accidental and not fundamental. Society could exist without it." [36]

Marx's thoughts led him to the view that exchange "corresponds to a definite mode of production." [37] Socialism, a non-commodity form of production, implies the absence of exchange relationships. Marx stated: "If labor is once again to be related to its objective conditions as to its property, another system must replace that of private exchange." [38] Engels agreed: "No society can permanently retain the mastery of its own production and the control over the social effects of its process of production unless it abolishes exchange between individuals." [39]

According to Marx and Engels all exchange (production for market or sale) is private or individual, because it takes place between autonomous units. In Marx's and Engels' sense, market socialism is private or individual exchange because the separate managers of state or publicly owned firms deal with each other and consumers through the market, and workers sell their labor power for wages.

PRIVATE PROPERTY

Marx concentrated his energy on the analysis of capitalism, which had evolved out of the dissolution of feudalism: "The economic structure of capitalistic society has grown out of the economic structure of feudal society. The dissolution of the latter set free the elements of the former." [40] Since capitalism presupposes the separation of laborers from property in the means of production, the process which clears the way for capitalism is the process through which the private property forms, wages and capital, evolve.

The mode of production establishes the rationality for the social division of labor and thereby determines property arrangements, since property rights cannot contradict the requirements of the mode of production. In the commodity mode of production, the division of labor receives its rationality from market exchange,* and the right to exchange property is required. In a non-commodity mode of production, the division of labor receives its rationality from social custom, as in a ritual economy, or from a social plan, as in communism, and only the right to use property is required. The property form, then, corresponds to the form of the social division of labor, and the form of the social division of labor is determined by the mode of production.

For example, if the mode of production is householding (the "Germanic" mode of production), the division of labor is within separate households producing for direct use. Each household contains within itself all conditions for production, and each member of a household has a claim to a portion of the household's product. To take another example, the

* "Division of labor in society is brought about by the purchase and sale of the products of different branches of industry." Marx, *Capital* I (New York: International Publishers, 1967), p. 355.

"Asiatic" mode of production is characterized by the self-sustaining unity of manufacture and agriculture within the village commune, and thus contains entirely within itself all conditions for production. The division of labor is within the village, and each member has a claim to a portion of the total product. But no one has exchange rights: no one can provision himself by buying and selling in markets. Thus, there is no private property: "The communal system on which this mode of production is based prevents the labor of an individual from becoming private labor and his product [from becoming] the private product of a separate individual." [41]

Exchange rights in property grow with exchange. If exchange is to develop within a non-exchange mode of production, there must be conditions favorable to exchange. These conditions are, according to Marx, least favorable in the Asiatic mode of production. The Asiatic mode resists exchange and thus "survives longest and most stubbornly. This is due to the fundamental principle on which it is based, that is, that the individual does not become independent of the community; that the circle of production is self-sustaining unity of agriculture and craft manufacture." [42] Since the individual's production is embodied in the community's production, exchange does not develop within the community. The despot appropriates the surplus product of the separate villages for his own use, so exchange does not develop between villages. Other modes of production, such as the "Ancient," allow more scope to exchange and private property, but, according to Marx, in these societies exchange never developed to the extent of producing capitalism. Even among the Greeks and Romans, the most advanced nations of antiquity, money "does not penetrate into all economic relations. For example, taxes in kind and deliveries in kind remained the basis of the Roman empire even at the height of its development; indeed a completely evolved monetary system existed in Rome only in the army, and it never permeated the whole complex of labor." [43]

According to Marx, when feudal lords dismissed their retainers, "a mass of free proletarians was hurled on the labor market." [44] But the "feudal lords created an incomparably larger proletariat by the forcible driving of the peasantry from the land, to which the latter had the same feudal rights as the lord himself, and by the usurpation of the common lands." [45] In this way feudal lords "vindicated for themselves the rights of modern private property in estates to which they had only a feudal title." [46] Marx says that this "expropriation is written in the annals of mankind in letters of blood and fire." [47]

Under feudalism large landowners did not mix their own labor with the land but exacted surplus labor (labor in excess of that needed for the maintenance and reproduction of the laborer) from the serf and peasant cultivators ("direct producers" in Marx's terminology) of their lands. Nevertheless, the exploited direct producers, from whom the landowner extracted surplus labor, possessed property rights in the means of production. They possessed property rights defined as *rights to use*. Such rights can perhaps be thought of as hereditary leases to land. Thus, although a feudal lord might sell land, those who possessed rights to use went with it. As long as production was not separate from use, the direct producers were secure in their possession of the land (that is, secure in their rights to use).

But as exchange developed, the form taken by the surplus labor that was appropriated by the lords changed from "labor rent" to "rent in kind" to "money-rent." [48] Once money-rent prevailed, "the traditional and customary legal relationship between landlord and subjects . . . is necessarily turned into a pure money relationship fixed contractually in accordance with the rules of positive law. . . . This transformation serves on the one hand, provided other general production relations permit, to expropriate more and more the old peasant possessors and to substitute capitalist tenants in their stead. On the other hand, it leads to the former possessor buying himself free from his rent obligation and to his transformation into an independent peasant with complete ownership of the land he tills." [49]

As exchange permeates the feudal community, feudal lords lose their rights to use a portion of the labor of the direct producers, and the latter lose their rights to use the land. With the destruction of the feudal community, there is a transformation in the form of property rights. Exchange rights in land "become essential factors," [50] and in general property rights take on the form of exchange rights. Individual exchange rights in property become vested in land, labor services, and capital. According to Marx, *individuals* do not *own* property until they have exchange rights in it. Marx defines *private property* in terms of the *right to exchange*.

Under feudalism, men were not divorced from the means of production. They did not have to maintain themselves by selling their labor services. Therefore, men did not conceive of exchange rights in labor services, or *wages*. There were some slaves who were bought and sold as commodities, but labor power was not a commodity. Marx wrote that "according to the conditions of production, property will take different forms." [51] As early as the *Economic and Philosophic Manuscripts,* Marx realized that wages are a private property form under capitalism: "wages and private property are identical," [52] that is, men have exchange rights in their labor power. Without wages, capitalism is not possible.

Marx's emphasis on private property as the result of the development of exchange, and on the relative absence of exchange in feudalism, is found throughout his writings. He states bluntly that "the capitalist mode of appropriation, the result of the capitalist mode of production, produces capitalist private property." [53] And he is not obscure when he writes: "We may see that the development of exchange and exchange value brings about the dissolution of labor's relations of property in its conditions of existence. . . . Production based on exchange value and a community based on the exchange of these exchange values . . . presuppose and produce the separation of labor from its objective conditions [means of production]." [54] In other words, "private property, as the antithesis to social, collective property, exists only where the means of labor [labor services] and the external conditions of labor [means of production] belong to private individuals." [55]

The enclosures were brought about by the growth of exchange. The development of the commodity mode of production required the reorganization of land toward producing exchange value for market rather than direct use-values for serf and lord. Thus change in the mode of production forced changes in property relations. The same process that caused the nobility to appropriate land as their private property produced the laborer's property rights in his labor services—that is, it created wage labor.

The feudal relation between lord and serf was one in which the lord appropriated surplus value (the value of surplus labor) from the serf and turned it into his property, but it was not an exchange relationship. The lord's appropriation of surplus value took the form of a direct use-value for his consumption. Thus, exploitation was limited by the lord's ability to consume use-values. As we shall see in the next chapter, the difference between feudal and capitalist exploitation is that the latter is not limited by the capitalist's ability to consume. Under capitalism a "boundless thirst" for surplus labor arises from the nature of production itself. Here we only want to emphasize that exchange was not a principal element in feudal production.

Marx points out that the feudal lord's appropriation of surplus labor took the form of obligations on the part of the serf which he met by payment of goods and services in kind. Marx writes that personal dependence forms the groundwork of feudal society and that in such a society "there is no necessity for labor and its products to assume a fantastic form different from their reality [that is, labor and its products do not take the commodity form]. They take the shape, in the transactions of society, of services in kind and payments in kind.

Here the particular and natural form of labor, and not, as in a society based on production of commodities, its general abstract form, is the immediate social form of labor." [56] He goes on to say that "no matter, then, what we may think of the parts played by the different classes of people themselves in feudal society, the social relations between individuals in the performance of their labor appear at all events as their own mutual personal relations, and are not disguised under the shape of social relations between the products of labor." [57] He says that an example of directly associated labor is "close at hand in the patriarchal industries of a peasant family that produces corn, cattle, yarn, linen, and clothing for home use. These different articles are, as regards the family, so many products of its labor, but as between themselves, they are not commodities." [58]

The development and extension of exchange produces the classes of laborer and capitalist; it produces exchange rights or private property in labor services and the means of production. There is no longer community, but a mass of private producers connected by exchange relationships through the market. Once labor has the form of wage labor and the means of production have the form of capital, "commodity production becomes the general form of production." [59]

SOCIALISM OR COMMUNISM *

Non-commodity modes of production are modes that are not based on exchange by mutually independent persons. Having outlined the nature of pre-capitalist non-commodity modes

---

* Robert C. Tucker, among others, has noted that "these two terms were always used by Marx and Engels more or less interchangeably." *The Marxian Revolutionary Idea* (New York: Norton, 1969), p. 4. The two terms were used interchangeably to denote a mode of social production that is not based on exchange.

of production, let us now examine the nature of the post-capitalist non-commodity mode of production.

It is well known that Marx never supplied the specifics of how socialism or communism would work out the plan that replaces market organization. However, he did define the organizational nature of socialism, which is characterized by the absence of the principal elements of commodity production. Under socialism or communism there would be no exchange between individuals, no money, no private property, no economic crises, and no alienation. There would be central economic planning. In fact, planning emerges as the single defining organizational characteristic of Marxian socialism or communism.

To Marx and Engels planning did not mean, as it generally means to modern writers, planning through markets. Rather, it meant the abolition of the market system. To them, unplanned production meant the separation of production from use, or commodity economy.

Throughout Marx's work communism is viewed as the transcendence of alienation. In *The German Ideology*, Marx connects the transcendence of alienation with planning. The market is an "alien force existing outside them [individuals], of the origin and end of which they are ignorant, which they thus cannot control." [60] Then he writes: "with the communistic regulation of production (and, implicit in this, the destruction of the alien relation between men and what they themselves produce), the power of the relation of supply and demand is dissolved into nothing and men get exchange, production, the mode of their mutual relation, under their own control again." [61]

In *Capital* Marx says that "the life process of society, which is based on the process of material production, does not strip off its mystical veil until it is treated as production by freely associated men, and is consciously regulated by them in accordance with a settled plan." [62] "Production by freely associated men" means production by men who are not independent of one another and who are not dominated by their own productive relations—that is, men who are free from domination by the market. It is a pervasive theme in Marx that under communism purposive social control takes the place of the autonomy of the market system.

The importance of central economic planning in Marx's concept of communism has been generally overlooked.* Marx mentioned the necessity for planning in most of his major works after *The German Ideology,* but it was never specially emphasized. However, the apparent antithesis of planning, the withering away of the state, is not emphasized either; yet many interpreters seem to place great importance on this aspect of communism. Marx mentions the abolition of the state in the *Manuscripts,* and this notion remains an element of communism throughout his work. The apparent contradiction between central economic planning and the withering away of the state is perhaps resolved by Engels in *Anti-Dühring:* "The interference of the state power in social relations becomes superfluous in one sphere after another, and then ceases of itself. The government of persons is replaced by the administration of things and the direction of the processes of production. The state is not 'abolished,' *it withers away.*" [63]

The "administration of things" means central economic planning. Engels says that "anarchy in social production is replaced by conscious organization on a planned basis." [64] That Marx and Engels believed that organization of social production can be achieved in the absence of government is not a mystery. According to them, under capitalism the government represents the class interests of the bourgeoisie, and its main

---

* Oscar J. Hammen has suggested to us that this defect may result from the fact that many scholars do not fully comprehend the term "organization of labor," as it was used occasionally by Marx and Engels and more extensively in socialistic literature in general, notably among the French. By "organization of labor" most people then meant a planned economy—namely the full organization of labor (in its broadest sense as all human effort), in contrast to the allegedly haphazard supply and demand relationships of the market.

function is in repressing the class interests of the proletariat. But under socialism there is *only one class,* so *agreement is possible.* Marx does not have the problem of reconciling individual interests—there are only class interests. So when there is a single class, there is a single interest.

Such is Marx's reasoning. His idea of a single class with a single interest is as utopian as his idea that a modern industrial society can dispense with exchange. Since Marx's writings are programmatic, the utopian aspects of his work were not confined to formal academic debate. Instead, his followers transformed them into a force in history. Roberts has referred to this force as "speculative excess." [65]

Marx believed that communism was the transcendence of alienation. He also believed that it was the acquisition of true freedom. According to Marx (and Engels), that is the freedom that is acquired by people collectively when they are able to control the society in which they live. The bourgeois freedom of contract is illusory. Marx wrote: "Thus, in imagination, individuals seem freer under the dominance of the bourgeoisie than before, because their conditions of life seem accidental; in reality, of course, they are less free, because they are more subjected to the violence of things [the anarchy of commodity exchange or markets]." [66]

Engels' famous phrase, "humanity's leap from the realm of necessity into the realm of freedom," [67] refers to the freedom acquired when men are able to "fashion their own history." The following quotation reveals the nature of freedom according to Engels (and Marx): "Freedom therefore consists in the control over ourselves and over external nature which is founded on knowledge of natural necessity; it is therefore necessarily a product of historical development." [68]

We see here the origins of the contemporary dispute between the Western point of view that there is more freedom in a society founded on democracy and market exchange and the Soviet point of view that finds freedom in control and planning. There are two completely different concepts of freedom involved. In the West, political and economic freedom generally mean the absence of coercion or limitations on individual choice. The Soviet view of freedom, originating with Marx and Engels, means freedom from autonomous forces and is a freedom that comes with the ability to control society's destiny. In the Marxian scheme, once men's lives are no longer subject to control by the market, society is no longer subject to the drift of history. It is man's control over things that signifies "the end of prehistory."

MARX'S TAXONOMY

It is helpful to set out formally Marx's classification of economic systems. It is in terms of the purposes of production, of which Marx acknowledges two: production for exchange, and production for direct use. Although economies may include both purposes, Marx's taxonomy depends upon which purpose is predominant.

According to Marx, the division of labor characterizes human existence and cannot be transcended, although its deleterious effects can be mitigated under communism because "society regulates the general production and thus makes it possible for me to do one thing today and another tomorrow." [69] Division of labor is therefore an element of all economies. Figure 1 illustrates Marxian theoretical taxonomy. Any economy must include either elements A and B but not C, or elements A and C but not B. The former is an economy of production for direct use, and the latter is a market economy. Thus, Marxian taxonomy makes no organizational differentiation between capitalism and market socialism. In a critique of Proudhon, Marx referred to market socialism as society "conceived as an abstract capitalist." [70]

Among the production for direct-use economies are found the Asiatic, ancient, and feudal economies and Marx's vision of the planned socialist economy. They share in common pro-

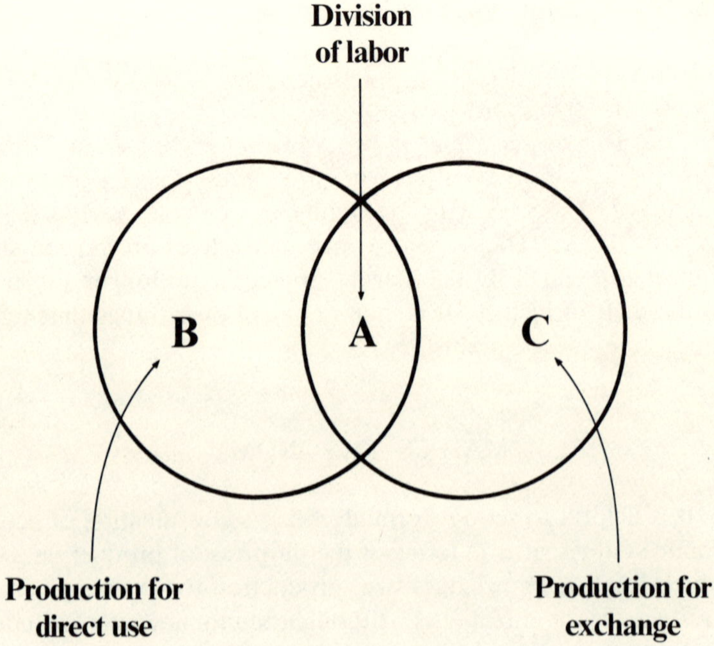

Marxian Taxonomy

Figure 1

duction for direct use and some elements of tradition, but they differ in the exercise of conscious will over economic life.

Marx's life work is a study of capitalist production, which he defined in terms of its unique characteristic. It is not division of labor and surplus labor that Marx finds unique to capitalism, but production for exchange on the market as the predominant mode of production.

Marx's taxonomy implies definite organizational forms. Throughout his writings Marx emphasizes the mutual independence of producers in a system of commodity production, the unplanned nature of commodity production, and its separation of production from use. In *Anti-Dühring* Engels emphasizes *"the organization of production in the individual factory"* as compared to *"the anarchy of production in society as a whole"* [71] and states: "The seizure of the means of production by society puts an end to commodity production, and therewith to the domination of the product over the producer. Anarchy in social production is replaced by conscious organization on a planned basis." [72]

Figure 2 indicates Marx's and Engels' concept of market organization. Each member or firm (*a, b, c, d, e,* and *f*) is mutually independent and related to each other member by a money payment in buying and selling that is guided by price and profit signals. The character of organization *between* members is polycentric. *Within* each member, however, there is the planned order of the factory organized by administratively specified allocation (drawn only for *a*). The character of organization of each individual member is hierarchic.

Instead of mutual independence, direct association characterizes all non-market economies. Direct association implies hierarchic order, and Marx's pre-capitalist economies certainly seem hierarchical, being organized under a family head, a feudal lord, or an oriental despot. Many think that Marx's concept of communism is nonhierarchical, but perhaps they have failed to understand Marx's idea of freedom

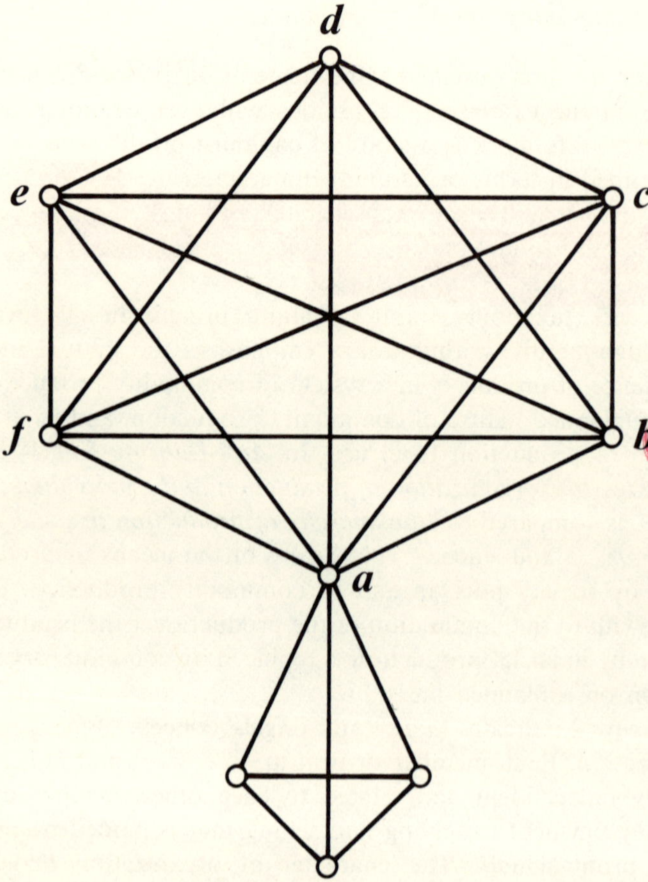

Market organization:
polycentric between
firms *(a–f),* hierarchic
within each firm *(a).*

Figure 2

under communism.* The organization of people under a plan implies hierarchy, and Lenin understood the post-capitalist Marxian society as one in which "the whole of society will have become one office and one factory." [73]

There is evidence that Marx entertained the utopian concept of a planned hierarchy subject to democratic control, in which peoples' places in the hierarchy changed as often as four times a day ("to hunt in the morning, fish in the afternoon, rear cattle in the evening, criticize after dinner").[74] This would seem to be a planned and ordered society in which the hierarchical levels are of no social or political significance. They would merely be the organizational expression of the directly associated producers.

Lenin's ideas, expressed in *The State and Revolution,* that everyone would take part in the administration of the state and all would be managers of the economy probably came from Marx, and Marx's notion that a person's place in the hierarchy would change frequently may have inspired the practice today in China and Cuba of expecting factory and office workers to work in the fields and to perform other designated services. Similarly, recent reports from China mention units of the Chinese army raising poultry and making pharmaceuticals. If Marx's ideas are the basis for these practices, then it is a mistake to think that they are simply a reflection of socialist egalitarianism—the desire to avoid a stratified social structure based on jobs. These practices may also be inspired by Marx's view that society can be organized like a gigantic factory, so that people can be shifted about from job to job in society in much the same way as they might be shifted from one department to another in a factory.

---

* As pointed out, Marx's concept of freedom, so far from relating to any notion of individual autonomy, means precisely society's liberation from autonomous forces, a freedom that comes with society's ability to control its own destiny.

— 3 —

Capital

"Capital is dead labor, that vampire-like, only lives by sucking living labor, and lives the more, the more labor it sucks." [1] Marx used less colorful language in the *Manuscripts,* where capital is said to be stored-up labor, the governing power over labor and its products, and private property in the products of other men's labor.[2]

As stored-up labor, capital has two forms, constant capital and variable capital. Constant capital, "which is represented by the means of production, by the raw materials, auxiliary material, and the instruments of labor, does not, in the process of production, undergo any quantitative alteration of value." [3] The value of the labor stored up in constant capital is transferred to a product during the production process without change in the magnitude of that value. Variable capital is the means of subsistence (or money that is used to buy the means of subsistence) paid to current labor. Variable capital, "represented by labor power, does, in the process of production, undergo an alteration of value." [4] Since according to

Marx current labor is the source of value, the use of variable capital can create new value (surplus value). Surplus value, when it is accumulated by the capitalist, becomes new capital which makes possible the employment of more workers.

Marx expressed the process that creates surplus value under capitalism by the symbols M-C-M′, where M represents money capital and C represents labor power. The capitalist uses money capital to purchase labor power which he uses to produce a commodity which he sells for a sum of money represented by M′.* M′ is greater than M, and the difference is surplus value which accrues to the capitalist.

The use of labor power creates surplus value because the value of the commodities produced is greater than the wage. Since according to Marx "the magnitude of the value of any article" is determined by "the amount of labor-time socially necessary for its production," the value of labor power is determined by the time required to produce the means of subsistence for a worker to live and reproduce. If it takes six hours work per day to produce the means of subsistence necessary to maintain and reproduce the worker, his wage is equal to the value of six hours production. But the capitalist will make him work longer, for example, ten hours a day. The additional four hours of work is termed surplus labor and yields a surplus product or surplus value.

Marx stated that "Capital is money: Capital is commodities." [5] This statement means two things: first, money becomes capital by purchasing labor power; and second, commodities are produced by the capitalist and sold for money so that the capitalist can again purchase labor power. Money received by the workers as wages enables them to purchase the means of subsistence (commodities). In effect, the money form of the means of subsistence is used to purchase labor power; so the means of subsistence are a form of capital.

---

* M′ is then used to purchase more labor power and becomes M (money capital) in a new sequence, M-C-M′.

Marx's concept of capital differs from that of the classicists in an important respect. Marx did not conceive of capital simply in terms of physical objects or as man-made aids to production. He said: "Capital is essentially a *capitalist;* but at the same time production in general is *capital,* as an element in the existence of the capitalist quite distinct from him. Thus we shall later find that in the term *capital* much is subsumed that does not apparently belong to the concept. E.g., capital is loaned. It is accumulated, etc. In all these relations it appears to be a mere object, and entirely to coincide with the matter of which it consists." [6]

In general, the classicists viewed capital as "mere objects," but Marx did not. For example, a machine may or may not be capital. What makes a machine capital, according to Marx, is the form of social organization in which the machine is employed. Marx wrote in a letter to P. V. Annenkov in 1846: "Lastly and in general, it is altogether absurd to make *machinery* an economic category alongside with division of labor, competition, credit, etc. Machinery is no more of an economic category than the ox which draws the plough. The application of machinery in the present day is one of the relations of our present economic system, but the way in which machinery is utilized is totally distinct from the machinery itself." [7]

Following Bohm-Bawerk, some economists see as capital anything that increases productivity by rendering production more roundabout.[8] Hence any economic system is capitalistic if it tends to use more capital-intensive (more roundabout) methods of production.* By Bohm-Bawerk's definition, capital is not something that distinguishes the socialist mode of production from commodity production. This is not what

---

* The hand-carving of wooden furniture would be a more direct and labor-intensive method of production than carving by machines, a roundabout and capital-intensive method. Instead of using labor to carve, it is used to make machines that carve—a "roundabout" method of production.

Marx meant by capital. According to Marx, capital is *"a relation of production."* [9] It exists only in a market economy. It is unique to commodity production. Marx chided other socialists for believing that socialism would keep capital but get rid of capitalists. In fairness to these socialists, they were probably using the classicists' or Bohm-Bawerk's concept of capital rather than Marx's. Marx is not noted for being receptive or sympathetic to concepts and opinions that differ from his own. Given Marx's view of capital as being a consequence of the form of social organization, "the concept of capital implies the capitalist." [10]

EXCHANGE AND THE FORMATION OF CAPITAL

The difference between Marx and other economists is that according to Marx, before anything can become capital it must first be a commodity and possess value in exchange. Therefore, exchange is a pre-condition for the existence of capital.

Money becomes capital when it is exchanged in the market for labor power. But before the development of the historical conditions for the exchange of money (as money capital) and labor power, money was exchanged for other products such as wheat, coats, and linen; so products of labor became commodities before labor services did. The commodity mode of production has a noncapitalist stage—the simple circulation of commodities.* This stage is symbolized by C-M-C, where the Cs represent various commodities and M is money. In this case, M is not money capital because it is not exchanged for labor power, only for products of labor. Marx emphasized

* Circulation of capital does not replace simple circulation of commodities. While the capitalist seeks exchange value through the process M-C-M′, the worker seeks use-value by selling his labor power in order to buy consumer goods, or C-M-C.

that the existence of markets or the circulation of money and commodities is not enough to define a system as capitalist. He said: "The historical conditions for its [capital's] existence are by no means given with the mere circulation of money and commodities. It can spring into life only when the owner of the means of production and subsistence meets in the market with the free laborer selling his labor-power. And this one historical condition comprises a world history. Capital, therefore, announces from its first appearance a new epoch in the process of social production." [11] When Marx says that capital is a "new epoch in the process of social production," he does not mean that it ushers in a new mode of production but that the child has grown into the adult. The adult (final) stage of commodity production commences when labor power becomes a commodity.

Marx recognized that money had existed in different forms of society, that is, in different modes of production, but prior to commodity production it could not be transformed into capital, and its role as the medium in which exchange values are established was limited because "deliveries in kind and labor services predominated over money payments and services remunerated by money." [12] Before the predominance of either simple commodity production or capitalism, an important use of money was as a hoard or a means to accumulate treasure. In a society where commodity exchange had not become widespread, money was synonymous with wealth and was hoarded.

Even after the advent of simple commodity production and capitalism, it is possible for some persons or families to become wealthy simply by accumulating as a treasure money earned from one's own labor or from selling the products of one's own labor. According to Marx, this is "so insignificant . . . that it is not worth mentioning historically." [13] Capitalistic wealth, which greatly exceeds even the hoards of feudal lords and princes, is possible only when money ceases to be used as a form of treasure and becomes a medium of exchange. The capitalist realizes that his wealth depends on the circulation of money instead of the hoarding of it.

It cannot be overemphasized that capital is based on exchange. "The circulation of commodities is the starting point of capital." [14] Marx saw the historical development of the market system in terms of the erosion of the feudal mode of production by the extension of exchange which gradually transformed the purpose of production. The existence of monetary wealth helped to create the conditions for the predominance of the commodity mode of production. Marx wrote:

> Admittedly, monetary wealth in the form of merchants' wealth had helped to accelerate and dissolve the old relations of production, and had, e.g., enabled the landowner to exchange his corn, cattle, etc., for imported use-values, instead of squandering his own production with his retainers, whose number, indeed, was to a large extent taken as the measure of his wealth. . . . Monetary wealth had given greater significance to the exchange-value of his revenue. . . . The evolution of exchange value is favored by the existence of *money* in the form of a social order of merchants. It dissolves a production whose object is primarily immediate use-value, and the forms of property which correspond to such production —the relation of labor to its objective conditions—thus giving an impetus to the creation of a *labor market*.[15]

Production for exchange in the market can exist on the periphery although a non-commodity mode of production (feudalism, for instance) predominates. But exchange inexorably erodes the system whereby obligations are met with goods and services in kind. Eventually market exchange predominates, and a society of persons directly associated in a form of community (the feudal manor) dissolves and is transformed into a society of mutually independent individuals. According to Engels, "money forces the commodity form even on the objects which have hitherto been produced for the producer's own use; it drags them into exchange." [16]

Although simple commodity production may exist for a long time before exchange becomes the general mode of production, that is, before the advent of capitalism, eventually labor power is "dragged into" exchange and becomes a commodity. The formation of capital is a consequence. The existing means of production and subsistence come to be exchanged in the market. When they are exchanged (by means of money) for labor power, they become a form of capital. Marx rejected the idea that capital originated as the result of some frugal individuals managing to accumulate some of the products of their labor which they used to employ others. On this matter he stated his views quite clearly:

> The *original formation of capital* does not, as is often supposed, proceed by the *accumulation* of food, tools, raw materials, or in short, of the *objective* conditions of labor detached from the soil and already fused with human labor. Not by means of capital creating the objective conditions of labor. Its *original* formation occurs simply because the historic process of the dissolution of an old mode of production, allows value existing in the form of *monetary wealth* to *buy* the objective conditions of labor on one hand, to exchange the *living* labor of the now free workers for money, on the other. All these elements are already in existence. What separates them out is a historic process, a process of dissolution, and it is *this* which enables money to turn into *capital.*[17]

He emphasized that the process of dissolution of the old mode of production results in use-values being transformed into exchange values:

> The means of subsistence formerly consumed by the lords and their retainers were now available for purchase by money, and money wished to purchase them in order through their instrumentality to purchase labor. Money had neither *created* nor *accumulated* these means of subsistence. They were already present, consumed and reproduced, before they

were consumed and reproduced through the intervention of money. The only change was that these means of production were now thrown on to the *exchange market*. They had now been detached from their immediate connection with the mouths of the retainers, etc., and transformed from use-values into exchange values, thus falling under the government and sovereignty of monetary wealth. The same applies to the instruments of labor.[18]

As the old mode of production dissolves and the existing means of subsistence and means of production are turned into commodities, the existing labor force is turned into a mass of free, propertyless workers.[19] They are propertyless in the sense that they have lost their traditional rights in the means of subsistence and the means of production. But they have acquired new property rights in their own labor power.

The feudal system began to decline with the spread of commercial activity and the rise of towns, and it was in towns that capital first concentrated. Unlike the manor, the town's purpose of production was for exchange. Capital appeared as a new property form based on exchange.* Marx wrote that "the separation of town and country can also be understood as the separation of capital and landed property, as the beginning of the existence and development of capital independent of landed property—the beginning of property having its basis only in labor and exchange." [20]

The landlord himself was transformed into a capitalist.[21] The sale of the manor's surplus means of subsistence to former serfs, who had moved to the towns, gradually transformed the purpose of the manor's production. Serfs who remained were gradually transformed into sellers of labor ser-

* Marx says that capital is both a property form and a relation of production. As pointed out, Marx defines private property in terms of the right to exchange. Thus capital is a property form because its owner possesses rights to exchange, and capital is a relation of production that exists when the worker and the capitalist exchange with each other.

vice for money wages, and the feudal lord was transformed into an agricultural capitalist. The manor's land was also drawn into exchange. When this happened it became a form of constant capital similar to machinery.* With the demise of the manor, it became possible for anyone to acquire, through purchase in the market, exchange rights in land.

The rising mercantile class in the towns did most to further the formation of capital. This class usually found itself in opposition to the guilds and crafts. The guilds were not an institution that furthered capital formation because their regulations usually limited the hiring of free labor and limited the use of machinery.[22] The crux of the matter is that the guilds were caught up in simple commodity production. According to Marx, "though urban crafts are based substantially on exchange and the creation of exchange values, the main object of production is not *enrichment* or *exchange value as exchange value,* but the *subsistence of man as an artisan, as a master-craftsman,* and consequently use-value. Production is therefore everywhere subordinate to a presupposed consumption, supply to demand, and its expansion is slow." [23]

ACCUMULATION

"Accumulate! Accumulate! That is Moses and the Prophets!" [24] Accumulation has always taken place through the transformation of surplus output into means of production, means of subsistence, and money hoards, but in pre-capitalist and post-capitalist modes of production, accumulation is not an end in itself. In capitalism, accumulation is an end in itself and takes place when the capitalist converts surplus value into new capital. The key to *capitalist* accumulation is commodity circulation. According to Marx:

* Strictly speaking, land that has been improved by labor is a form of capital.

> The restless never-ending process of profit-making alone is what he [the capitalist] aims at. This boundless greed after riches, this passionate chase after exchange value, is common to the capitalist and the miser; but while the miser is merely a capitalist gone mad, the capitalist is a rational miser. The never-ending augmentation of exchange value, which the miser strives after by seeking to save his money from circulation, is attained by the more acute capitalist by constantly throwing it afresh into circulation.[25]

Capital accumulation has no limits, because in the commodity mode of production surplus labor is transformed into exchange values. Exchange value is an abstract form of wealth, and also the social form of wealth in the commodity mode of production. It is wealth created by man as a consequence of a particular social organization and has no natural limit. Since capital is always viewed by the capitalist as a form of exchange value, "the circulation of capital has therefore no limits."[26] In contrast, the accumulation of surplus labor in the form of use-values is limited by the ability of the exploiter to consume.

The purpose of production on a feudal manor was use-values or consumption. If the lord did accumulate, he accumulated money and products as a hoard with an eye toward future consumption. The capitalist is different. The capitalist consumes use-values but his own consumption is not the purpose of his production. "Use-values must therefore never be looked upon as the real aim of the capitalist."[27] And it makes no sense for the capitalist to hoard commodities as use-values, since this would prevent him from accumulating capital. Marx says that for a capitalist "accumulation of a hoard in the shape of commodities would be sheer tomfoolery."[28]

Marx acknowledged his debt to Aristotle for the idea that there is a limitation to wealth in the form of use-value but no limitation to wealth in the form of exchange value.[29] It is clear that Marx derived (at least partly) his view of the commodity mode of production and the separation between exchange value and use-value from Aristotle's view of commercial activity. As we emphasize, Marx saw the end of capitalism (and the commodity mode of production) as the end of market exchange. Abolishing market exchange would, *inter alia,* eliminate the basis for endless accumulation. In Marxian socialism, accumulation as an end in itself cannot take place because only use-values are produced. Marx does not suggest that the private accumulation of wealth under socialism would cease simply because there is no private property in the means of production. The absence of private property in the means of production does not strike at the heart of the matter. Socialism is characterized by the absence of the value form that permits endless accumulation to take place.

EXPLOITATION

The purpose of the capitalist *qua* capitalist is not the consumption of surplus value. Such consumption would encroach on his ability to accumulate capital. The capitalist is not concerned with the use-value of commodities, only with their exchange value; but he is very much concerned with the use-value of labor power. The capitalist extracts labor from the worker; he consumes labor power.[30] Exploitation occurs when the capitalist extracts more labor from each worker than is required for the subsistence of each worker and his family. In other words, the capitalist appropriates the surplus labor.

Exploitation is usually viewed as appropriating the products of labor, and this does happen. In the commodity mode of production, these products are commodities that have exchange values; so it appears that the capitalist appropriates some of the exchange values that should rightfully belong to the worker. But such an approach does not lead one to see the true nature of exploitation in Marx's system. Exploitation is really the extraction of use-value beyond what is necessary to maintain and reproduce the worker—the use-value of labor time under capitalism, the use-value of the serf's labor under feudalism, the use-value of the slave's labor in some ancient mode of production, and the use-value of labor by the community under socialism. Therefore exploitation is not unique to capitalism or the commodity mode of production.

What is unique to capitalism is the way in which exploitation takes place. According to Marx, the patriarchal relationship between journeyman and master in the guilds is replaced by the monetary relationship between worker and capitalist.[31] Under capitalism, an exchange of labor power for money takes place before an exploitation of labor occurs. The capitalist must buy labor power (the worker's time) before he can extract labor (the use of labor power) from the worker. Because the capitalist is able to extract labor, he is able to exploit the worker. In this regard the capitalist is no different from the feudal lord who extracts labor from his serfs. The difference lies in the way the capitalist acquires command over the worker's time. Under feudalism the worker's time was available to the lord in accordance with traditional obligations. Under capitalism, the worker has no obligation to the capitalist until a money wage has been given in exchange for his labor power.

Exchange is not the cause of exploitation. Marx rejected the view of other socialists such as William Thompson and John F. Bray that exploitation results from unjust exchange because the worker does not receive what is rightfully his in the bargain.[32] According to Marx, the worker is not cheated in the market. He receives the exchange value of his labor power. Exploitation takes place after exchange, because what the capitalist has received as his part of the bargain is command over labor time. It takes place in the factory, where capitalist and worker are no longer equals as they were in the market but master and servant. The capitalist "now strides in front . . . the possessor of labor-power follows as his laborer. The one with an air of importance, smirking, intent on business; the other timid and holding back, like one who is bringing his own hide to market and has nothing to expect but—a hiding." [33]

Exploitation is intensified under capitalism. It is worse than it was under earlier modes of production, because although the capitalist extracts the use-value of labor power, he wants the exchange value of the products of labor. As pointed out, exchange value can be accumulated without limit, and since the accumulation of capital becomes an end in itself, the capitalist is driven to seek more and better ways to increase his extraction of surplus value. In a society where use-values predominate there is also exploitation, but it is limited because the accumulation of use-value is limited to amounts the exploiter can consume. It is otherwise in a society where exchange value predominates. In Marx's words:

> It is, however, clear that in any given economic formation of society, where not the exchange value but the use-value of the product predominates, surplus labor will be limited by a given set of wants which may be greater or less, and that here no boundless thirst for surplus labor arises from the nature of the production itself. Hence in antiquity over-work becomes horrible only when the object is to obtain exchange value in its specific independent money form—in the production of gold and silver.[34]

In feudal society just as in capitalist society, the extracted surplus value becomes the property of the exploiter. In communist society, extracted surplus value becomes communal property.

Marx did not approve of exploitation when the extracted surplus value becomes the private property of the exploiter. But Marx's condemnation of capitalism is stronger than his condemnation of feudalism. This stronger condemnation reflects more than the fact that capitalist exploitation is more intensive. Exploitation is milder in feudalism and communism because exchange value is absent. It is the presence of exchange value in capitalist society that allows surplus value to take an abstract (money) form and be accumulated without limit. In feudal and communist society surplus value takes the form of specific use-values (for example, grain).

When labor produces specific use-values, social labor takes particular concrete and natural forms. When labor produces exchange value or commodities, the social form of labor becomes abstract. Marx says that when production is for direct use, as in feudal society, "there is no necessity for labor and its products to assume a fantastic form different from their reality. They take the shape, in the transactions of society, of services in kind and payments in kind. Here the particular and natural form of labor, and not, as in a society based on production of commodities, its general abstract form, is the immediate social form of labor."[35]

Marx points out that although feudal society is exploitative, since social labor does not take an abstract or commodity form, the products of men's hands do not acquire a life of their own, and the mutual relations of the producers do not appear as a social relation between the products of their labor (that is, there is no "fetishism of commodities"): "No matter, then, what we may think of the parts played by the different classes of people themselves in this [feudal] society, the social relations between individuals in the performance of their labor appear at all events as their own mutual personal relations, and are not disguised under the shape of social relations between the products of labor."[36]

This makes it clear that Marx's condemnation of capitalism is not based solely on the intensity of exploitation and the fact that extracted surplus value becomes the private property of the exploiter. Rather, his condemnation is based on the social form of labor, and therefore on the form of social organization that results when the purpose of production is exchange.

The capitalist may increase his extraction of surplus value by lengthening the working day or by forcing the worker to work harder, but his attempts will be limited by the lessened efficiency of the labor force, and the wise capitalist knows that he must husband his machinery, land, and labor resources because they are necessary for continuing production.[37] The principal way for the capitalist to increase surplus value is to introduce technological improvements. A technological improvement in the consumer goods industries reduces the labor time necessary to produce the subsistence for the worker and his family. Therefore, with no change in the length of the working day, more labor is available to create surplus value for the capitalist. There is always inducement for the capitalist to introduce labor-saving technological improvements in his firm in order to reduce the size of his wage bill. Until others duplicate the technological improvement, the capitalist will receive a larger surplus value than his competitors.

Although technological change is not unique to capitalism, the social organization of capitalism, which engenders a "boundless thirst for surplus labor," promotes changes in technology far greater than any that had occurred under other modes of production. Rapid technological change is a consequence of the capitalist's drive to accumulate exchange values by exploiting labor. Technological change reduces the quantity of society's labor resources necessary to maintain the labor force, thus increasing surplus labor. And technological change, by constantly throwing workers out of jobs, keeps the wage rate at the socially determined minimum necessary to support the worker and his family; so workers are seldom able to collect any surplus output for themselves. Presumably, under socialism, the introduction of technology would be controlled by central economic planning. Instead of technology being introduced to increase the surplus value received by individual capitalists, it would be introduced to enhance the surplus value collected by the community.

Some see technology as the basis of the different modes of production, and have described Marx as a technological determinist. There is, in fact, some evidence in Marx's early work to suggest that he thought that technology determines the mode of production. For example, in *Poverty of Philosophy* (1847), he wrote: "Social relations are closely bound up with productive forces. In acquiring new productive forces men change their mode of production; and in changing their mode of production, in changing the way of earning their living, they change all their social relations. The handmill gives you society with the feudal lord; the steam-mill, society with the industrial capitalist." [38] And in the *Communist Manifesto* (1848), he said that "the bourgeoisie cannot exist without constantly revolutionizing the instruments of production, and thereby the relations of production, and with them the whole relations of society." [39]

However, in the later *Grundrisse* (1857–58) Marx attempts to establish the foundations for social change. Modes of production are defined in terms of social organization, so that what is emphasized about capitalism is exchange. The emphasis on exchange is maintained throughout *Capital*.

— 4 —

Value and Crises

According to Marx, exchange, the principal characteristic of the commodity mode of production, is also the principal flaw in that mode of production. Because exchange is interposed between production and use, periodic crises occur. Marx believed that an economic system based on the separation of production from use was characterized by unplanned and uncoordinated interactions of mutually independent individuals (consumers, workers, and firms) and thereby inherently unstable. He thought that such an economic system had viability problems.*

The idea that the "anarchy of the market" caused the capitalist system to be crisis-prone was shared with Marx by early nineteenth-century socialists and by Engels, who offered insights in his 1844 essay, "Outlines of the Critique of Political Economy." Marx decided that crises are an inherent feature

---

* We are not concerned in this analysis with the "breakdown controversy." It is immaterial for our purposes whether the capitalist system destroys itself or is overthrown in a violent revolution.

of capitalism before he developed his economic analysis. In the *Manuscripts,* the theory of value is not developed; there is no theory of surplus value or the circulation of capital, but there is the idea that crises are the result of the unplanned operations of the market. In the *Manuscripts* Marx cited Wilhelm Schulz, who stated that there could be no possibility of permanence for a worker's income "in the anarchy of so-called free competition, with its ever-recurring fluctuations and periods of stagnation." [1] In the same work, Marx cited the French socialist Constantin Pecquer, who wrote:

> Competition is merely the expression of the freedom to exchange. . . . The right to use and abuse, freedom of exchange, and arbitrary competition—these three economic moments, which form one unit, entail the following consequences: each produces what he wishes, as he wishes, when he wishes, where he wishes, produces well or produces badly, produces too much or not enough, too soon or too late, at too high a price or too low a price; none knows whether he will sell, how he will sell, when he will sell, where he will sell, to whom he will sell. And it is the same with regard to purchases. The producer is ignorant of needs and resources, of demand and supply. . . . The supply does not know the demand, and the demand does not know the supply. You produce, trusting to a taste, a fashion, which prevails amongst the consuming public. But by the time you are ready to deliver the commodity, the whim has already passed and has settled on some other kind of product. . . . The inevitable consequences: bankruptcies occurring permanently and universally; miscalculations, sudden ruin and unexpected fortunes, commercial crises, unemployment, periodic gluts or shortages; instability and depreciation of wages and profits, the loss of enormous waste of wealth, time, and effort in this arena of fierce competition.[2]

Marx also quotes Adam Smith's discussion of how the accumulation of capital greatly improves the productive powers of workers, and then comments that over-production results.[3]

In his "Outlines of a Critique of Political Economy" Engels states, with an economy of words not usually found in his collaborator's writings, the cause, consequence, and cure for economic crises. However involved Marx's discussion of crises became, he never diverged significantly from the views expressed by Engels. In Engels' words:

> The law of competition is that demand and supply always strive to complement the other, and therefore never do so. . . . The economist comes along with his lovely theory of demand and supply, proves to you that "one can never produce too much," and practice replies with trade crises, which reappear as regularly as comets, and of which we have now on the average one every five to seven years. For the last eighty years these trade crises have come just as regularly as the great plagues did in the past—and they have brought in their train more misery and more immorality than the latter. . . . If the producers as such knew how much the consumers required, if they were to organize production, if they were to share it out amongst themselves, then the fluctuations of competition and its tendency to crisis would be impossible.[4]

Thus, according to Engels, the unplanned nature of the market is the cause of crises; the cure is for producers to organize production. In other words, Marx and Engels believed that crises would not occur when there is central economic planning. Engels proceeds to argue that since the market is by its own nature unplanned, crises will continue to occur under capitalism until that system collapses (or is overthrown):

> But as long as you continue to produce in the present unconscious, thoughtless manner, at the mercy of chance, for just so long trade crises will remain; and each successive crisis is bound to become more universal and therefore worse than the preceding one; is bound to impoverish a larger body of small capitalists, and to augment in increasing proportion the numbers of that class who live by labor alone, thus visibly enlarging the mass of labor to be employed (the major prob-

> lem of our economists) and finally causing a social revolution such as has never been dreamt of by the school of wisdom of the economists.[5]

Marx describes crises at some length in his own words in *The Poverty of Philosophy* (1847). He says that crises occur in a modern industrial society because it is impossible to maintain the "true proportion between supply and demand" in an exchange economy.[6] Before the predominance of capitalism, demand came before supply. "Production followed close on the heels of consumption." [7] But in a society based on exchange there is "anarchy of production," and supply is produced without knowledge of demand. According to Marx, "individual exchange is suited only to small-scale industries of past centuries." [8] In order to have "progress without anarchy" in a modern industrial state, "you must abandon individual exchange." [9]

THE POSSIBILITY OF CRISES

The fact that a commodity must possess both use-value and exchange value opens up the possibility of economic crises.[10] As pointed out, exchange value is the market "form of value." In order to have value, goods must be produced by socially necessary human labor. But in a commodity economy, the existence of value in goods is revealed only when those goods are exchanged. Exchange, in effect, certifies that the labor time expended on any quantity of goods is socially necessary labor time. That is, it certifies that a social (market) demand does exist for goods. Goods are demanded in order to be consumed as use-values. If the goods are consumed as use-values (by being sold at prices proportional to their values), then the labor time expended to produce them is socially useful labor. Since goods are not produced for direct use, the determination that the labor expended is socially useful is made only after the goods are brought to market.

Labor expended on the production of goods that have no market is not socially necessary labor. From the standpoint of society (and the capitalist), it is wasted labor. According to Marx, because of the unplanned nature of capitalist production, there is a high probability that any producer will find that there is no market for at least some of his goods. It can happen that instead of having unsold goods, a producer will be able to sell his goods but at a price lower than their value. Marx saw no difference between these two results. In either case, some of the labor expended is socially unnecessary. For example, if a producer finds that 30 per cent of his goods are unsold (not exchanged), then 30 per cent of the labor expended to produce them is socially unnecessary. If the price of all of his goods fell by 30 per cent below their value, then 30 per cent of the labor expended on each good is wasted, and when all goods are sold 30 per cent of the total labor expended is wasted.

In production for direct use, there is no possibility of labor being socially unnecessary. When an individual produces for himself, for his family, for a primitive tribe, or for a communal society, he produces for a predetermined use—one determined in advance by the social arrangements within the family, tribe, or community. Hence the labor expended is socially useful; none of it is wasted as a result of too much or the wrong things being produced. According to Marx, the same holds true for a socialist economy. From Marx's standpoint, the role of central economic planning—a role that is not generally understood—is to bring about production for direct use in a modern industrial economy. Thus its role is to ensure that all labor expended is socially necessary labor.

It follows from the logic of Marx's analysis that any economy characterized by production for direct use will be immune to crises. Engels believed that crises began occurring about 80 years before he wrote "Outlines of a Critique of Political Economy." [11] Apparently he believed that prior to that time market exchange was not sufficiently widespread—there were still many types of production for direct use—for crises to occur.

Although Marx associated economic crises and the collapse of capitalism with industrialized countries, his emphasis is on exchange, not on industrialization per se. Once commodity production predominates, crises can originate in any sector of the economy. Since the crucial factor is the prevalence of exchange and not industry, there is no conflict between Marx's theory and a Marxian revolution occurring in an agricultural nation.*

THE LAW OF VALUE

Marx began his analysis in *Capital* by assuming that commodities are exchanged in proportion to the socially necessary labor time embodied in them. For example, if twenty yards of linen are exchanged for one coat, then one coat contains twenty times the socially necessary labor time contained in one yard of linen. This assumption means that in theory labor is so distributed among the different commodities that each commodity is produced in exactly the quantity demanded by society. If this condition were met in practice there would be no socially unnecessary labor (no wasted labor), and commodities would be produced in their correct *proportions*.

According to Marx, the "law of value of commodities ultimately determines how much of its disposable working time society can expend on each particular class of commodities."[12] In a society of mutually independent individuals, the law of value regulates the proportions of labor power allocated to the production of the various commodities. In

---

* Oscar J. Hammen points out that Marx and Engels both saw the revolutionary potential of agrarian elements. See Hammen, "Marx and the Agrarian Question," *American Historical Review*, Vol. 77, No. 3 (June 1972), pp. 679–704.

contrast, in a factory the division of labor is determined by the command of the capitalist.[13] When the division of labor in society is proportional to the social demand for various commodities, "then the products of various groups are sold at their values . . . or at prices which are certain modifications of these values or prices of production determined by general laws.*

The law of value regulates the allocation of labor among industries rather than among individual capitalists. In general, Marx assumed that within each industry, competition ensured that individual firms would be more or less homogeneous with respect to the labor required to produce a given output. Thus Marx stated that the law of value applies "not with reference to individual commodities or articles, but to each total product of the particular social spheres of production." [14]

In practice, commodities do not exchange in proportion to their values. Marx, as an economic theorist, assumed for the purpose of his analysis that they do, but only to show why in fact they do not. Marx's law of value really works by means of the deviation of price from value.[15] He wrote:

> Every individual article, or every definite quantity of a commodity may, indeed, contain no more than the social labor required for its production, and from this point of view the market value of this entire commodity represents only necessary labor, but if this commodity has been produced in excess of the existing social needs, then so much of the social

---

* Karl Marx, *Capital* III (New York: International Publishers, 1967), p. 635. The term "prices of production" was introduced by Marx in volume III of *Capital* when he was trying to solve the problem of transforming values into relative prices. Prices of production are different from labor values when the organic composition of capital (the ratio of machinery to labor) is different in different industries. Disproportionality results in market price diverging from both value and price of production. Since our concern is with disproportionality, we will ignore the difference between value and price of production. Usually, we will say that disproportionality results in market price diverging from value. This is equivalent to Marx's occasional phrasing that market prices diverge from prices of production.

> labor time is squandered and the mass of the commodity comes to represent a much smaller quantity of social labor in the market than is actually incorporated in it. (It is only where production is under the actual, predetermining control of society that the latter establishes a relation between the volume of social labor time applied in producing definite articles and the volume of the social want to be satisfied by these articles.) For this reason, these commodities must be sold below their market value, and a portion of them may even be altogether unsaleable.[16]

The law of value tries to ensure that labor is divided in the proper proportion. It has the same job in a society of independent producers that central planning has in a socialist society. According to Marx, it works to ensure the proper social division of labor by means of price fluctuations and crises. If too much labor is employed in the production of one product and too little in another, the price of the former will fall and the price of the latter will rise. But instead of price fluctuations smoothly restoring equilibrium (the proper proportion of labor among the products), Marx said that "violent price fluctuations therefore cause interruptions, great collisions, even catastrophes, in the process of reproduction." [17] Marx saw crises as the way in which the capitalist system restored equilibrium. In a crisis, the value of commodities (especially those commodities that function as capital) is destroyed.[18] Crises show that the social division of labor was not in the proper proportion, and by destroying values they bring about the proper proportion. Thus the basic reason for all crises is disproportionality.* In Marx's words:

> To say that there is no general over-production, but rather a disproportion within the various branches of production, is

---

* Some have turned Marx into an under-consumptionist, but Sowell realizes that disproportionality is the only source of crises in Marx. See Thomas Sowell, "Marx's *Capital* after One Hundred Years," *The Canadian Journal of Economics,* XXXIII, No. 1 (February 1967), pp. 57–58.

> no more than to say that under capitalist production the proportionality of the individual branches of production springs as a continual process from disproportionality, because the cohesion of the aggregate production imposes itself as a blind law upon the agents of production, and not as a law which, being understood and hence controlled by their common mind, brings the productive process under their joint control.[19]

Engels stated that "the law of value is precisely the fundamental law of commodity production, hence also of its highest form, capitalist production." [20] The law of value applies only to the commodity mode of production. In former modes of production, the division of labor in society was established by tradition or by command. In a socialist mode of production, the law of value would be superceded by central economic planning.[21]

According to Marx, the law of value can succeed in regulating the allocation of labor to the production of various commodities without the concomitant occurrence of crises only in the early stages of the commodity mode of production. In *The Poverty of Philosophy,* Marx said that "individual exchange is suited only to the small-scale industry of past centuries with its corollary of true proportion." [22]

In Volume I of *Capital,* Marx assumed that commodities exchange in proportion to the labor embodied in them. But in Volume III, when the organic composition of capital (the ratio of constant capital to variable capital, or alternatively, the ratio of machinery to labor) varies from industry to industry, commodities do not exchange in proportion to the labor embodied in them. This is the Marxian "transformation problem" about which much has been written.[23]

Marx was not able (indeed, it is impossible) to transform values into relative prices under the conditions laid down in Volume III (the organic composition of capital varies from industry to industry). The labor theory of value simply cannot yield a theory of relative prices. This has no consequences for our analysis of Marx's system, but concern about it has led many to miss the main thrust of Marx's analysis. Marx's "law of value" is not what economists mean by value theory; it is not a theory of price. As pointed out, the principal function of Marx's law of value is to regulate the social division of labor in a market system: if there is a disproportionate allocation of labor among various commodities, market prices will diverge from labor values. This statement is still valid even if Marx was not able to transform labor values into relative prices. Even if labor is not the only factor affecting price, it is usually the most important element in the cost of production; so too much or too little labor (and therefore too much or too little output) will result in price fluctuations. In Volume III, Marx continued to say that "the law of value dominates price movements with reductions or increases in required labor time making prices of production fall or rise." [24]

If it is admitted that other factors of production affect price, the logic of Marx's discussion of disproportionality is not impaired. The capitalist system could have been characterized by chronic disproportionality in the kinds of machinery and entrepreneurship and in the uses of land, as well as in labor. Price fluctuations, which Marx considered to be prima facie evidence that labor is not being divided in correct proportions, can also be considered evidence that other factors of production are not being allocated properly in the production of various commodities. Marx's statement that values which are created by labor are destroyed in a crisis would have to be modified only to indicate that other factors also create value. Our conclusion is that Marx's discussion of disproportionality is based on his analysis of exchange and does not rely on the labor theory of value as a theory of price. Marx's failure to solve the "transformation problem" is inconsequential for the problem of crises caused by disproportionality.

THE ANATOMY OF A CRISIS

In its most general form, a crisis may be said to occur whenever economic values are destroyed. Thus a crisis occurs whenever goods are unsold or sold at market prices below their values. A crisis occurs for an individual capitalist if he is unable to sell his product or is able to sell it only at a loss in value; it occurs for an individual worker if he is unable to sell his labor power. The capitalist system is always beset by small, individual crises, because the separation of production from use (unplanned production) always results in some disproportionality. But as pointed out, Marx was concerned with whether or not labor is allocated to different industries in the proper proportion. If it is not, then there are crises in some industries. Values are destroyed and the misallocated labor is wasted. If disproportionality becomes widespread, the economy as a whole is in a crisis.

As pointed out, the possibility of crises is created by the separation of production from use that characterizes exchange. The probability of crises increases as more and more products become commodities and are drawn into the market system. Money—the cash nexus—mediates between producer and consumer. Money, when it purchases labor power and becomes money capital, mediates between worker and employer. The role of money is central in Marx's analysis of crises. Marx says that although the circulation of money can occur without crises, "crises cannot occur without circulation of money." [25]

Before the advent of the commodity mode of production, money served principally as a hoard. Money had use-value as a store of value—a means to accumulate treasure. In the commodity mode of production, money has use-value as a medium in which exchange value is expressed. Marx said that "the commodity which has been set apart as the universal equivalent [money] is now an object which satisfies a universal need arising from the exchange process itself, and has the same use-value for everyone—that of being a carrier of exchange value or a universal medium of exchange." [26]

Marx said, "As a *measure of value,* and as a *standard of price,* money has two entirely distinct functions to perform." [27] When money functions as a measure of value, it serves as a measure of the human labor expended to produce a commodity. The capitalist, who knows how much labor was expended, hopes to receive an amount of money equal in value to the labor expended. Price is the actual amount of money a capitalist receives when he sells a commodity. It may be greater or less than the magnitude of a commodity's value in terms of the labor expended.[28] Marx stated that "price is the money-name of the labor realized in a commodity." [29]

If money served only as a measure of value, then prices would simply be a reflection of the quantity of socially necessary labor in an ounce of gold relative to the socially necessary labor time in various commodities. Money would become a form of labor certificate. But Marx clearly rejected this line of reasoning. Money does not directly represent labor time.[30] How much money is given in exchange for a commodity does not depend on the labor time required to produce that money.[31] How much money is given in exchange is determined "by the law of supply and demand only." [32]

Because of the dual function of money, the disproportionality inherent in the commodity mode of production takes the form of a divergence of money price from labor value. Marx wrote:

> Magnitude of value expresses a relation of social production, it expresses the connection that necessarily exists between a certain article and the portion of the total labor-time of society required to produce it. As soon as magnitude of value is converted into price, the above necessary relation takes the shape of a more or less accidental exchange ratio between a

> single commodity and another, the money-commodity. But this exchange ratio may express either the real magnitude of that commodity's value, or the quantity of gold deviating from that value, for which, according to circumstances, it may be parted with. The possibility, therefore, of quantitative incongruity between price and magnitude of value, or the deviation of the former from the latter, is inherent in the price-form itself. This is no defect, but, on the contrary, admirably adapts the price-form to a mode of production whose inherent laws impose themselves only as the mean of apparently lawless irregularities that compensate one another.[33]

Although it is possible for a general crisis to occur as a result of the circulation of commodities (C-M-C) if the interval between the sale of commodities, C-M, and the purchase of commodities, M-C, becomes too long,[34] Marx's analysis of crises is predicated upon the circulation of capital (M-C-M). However, crises for individuals occur all the time when there is simple circulation of commodities, because labor values are continually being destroyed in the case of individual producers who misjudge the market.[35]

Two conditions that amplify crises are the existence of credit and the development of wholesaling. Credit exists because money serves as a means of payment (standard of price).[36] Credit makes it possible to lengthen the interval between the sale of a commodity, C-M, and the purchase of another commodity, M-C. Credit may hide disproportionality, because goods may be produced and purchased with credit instead of hard cash. A chain of credit obligations develops. There are "debts due to A from B, to B from C, to C from A, and so on." [37] But disproportionality is not hidden for long. "The quantity of money current and the mass of commodities circulating during a given period, such as a day, no longer correspond," and "the debts contracted each day, and the payments falling due on the same day, are quite incommensurable quantities." [38] Debts can no longer be honored and the whole chain of obligations collapses. No one is willing or able to buy commodities. Money—hard cash—alone is demanded. Everyone wants money and no one wants to spend it; so money ceases to perform its function as a medium of exchange. Marx wrote:

> This confusion and stagnation paralyzes the function of money as a medium of payment, whose development is geared to the development of capital and is based on those presupposed price relations. The chain of payment obligations due at specific dates is broken in a hundred places. The confusion is augmented by the attendant collapse of the credit system, which develops simultaneously with capital, and leads to violent and acute crises, to sudden and forcible depreciations, to the actual stagnation and disruption of the process of reproduction, and thus to a real falling off in reproduction.[39]

The fact of disproportionality may also be hidden temporarily by the existence of wholesalers. The break in the circulation of commodities does not become immediately apparent once wholesaling has become widespread. Marx says that "mass production can have no other direct buyer, apart from other industrial capitalists, than the wholesaler." [40] Because wholesalers are buying from producers while consumers are not buying from retailers, inventories build up. Marx describes the ensuing events:

> Now one stream of commodities follows another, and finally it is discovered that the previous streams had been absorbed only apparently by consumption. The commodity-capitals compete with one another for a place in the market. Latecomers, to sell at all, sell at lower prices. The former streams have not yet been disposed of when payment for them falls due. Their owners must declare their insolvency or sell at any price to meet their obligations. This sale has nothing whatever to do with the actual state of demand. It only concerns

> the *demand for payment,* the pressing necessity of transforming commodities into money. Then a crisis breaks out. It becomes visible not in the direct decrease of consumer demand, the demand for individual consumption, but in the decrease of exchanges of capital for capital, of the reproductive process of capital.[41]

Since social demand in a commodity economy can be expressed only through money, disproportionality in one sector or industry may cause disproportionality in another sector. If there is disproportionality in commodities, there is disproportionality in the allocation of labor to the production of commodities. Unemployment and a fall in wages result. The reduction in wages and the unemployment reduce the consuming power of the workers, but this is a result and not the cause of crises.

Although there are statements in Marx that suggest an under-consumptionist view of crises, the thrust of his analysis emphasizes disproportionality. In Volume II of *Capital,* Marx explicitly rejected an under-consumptionist explanation:

> It is sheer tautology to say that crises are caused by the scarcity of effective consumption, or of effective consumers. . . . But if one were to attempt to give this tautology the semblance of a profounder justification by saying that the working class receives too small a portion of its own product and the evil would be remedied as soon as it receives a larger share of it and its wages increase in consequence, one could only remark that crises are always prepared by precisely a period in which wages rise generally and the working class actually gets a larger share of that part of the annual product which is intended for consumption. From the point of view of these advocates of sound and "simple" (!) common sense, such a period should rather remove the crisis. It appears, then, that capitalist production comprises conditions independent of good or bad will, conditions which permit the working class to enjoy that relative prosperity only momentarily, and at that always only as the harbinger of a coming crisis.[42]

The under-consumptionist explanation of crises implies that crises could be eliminated by reforms altering the distribution of income *within a commodity economy*. This, of course, does not sit well with a theory of revolution predicated on contradictions in the mode of production. The disproportionality explanation makes it clear that crises cannot be overcome unless the separation of production from use, which causes disproportionality, is overcome. By sticking to his guns on disproportionality, Marx was sticking to his theory of revolution based on contradictions in the mode of production. The problem, according to Marx, is not that "too much wealth is produced," but "too much wealth is produced in its capitalistic, self-contradictory forms." [43]

— 5 —

Distribution

According to Marx and Engels, distribution is determined by the mode of production. Distribution of the means of consumption reflects the distribution of the means of production, and the latter distribution reflects the social organization of production. Marx made this point in several of his works. In *Capital* he wrote that wages presuppose wage labor and profits presuppose capital. "These definite forms of distribution thus presuppose definite social characteristics of production conditions, and definite social relations of production agents. The specific distribution relations are thus merely the expression of the specific historical production relations." [1] In a manuscript written in 1857–58 but unpublished in his lifetime, he wrote: "The structure of distribution is entirely determined by the structure of production. Distribution itself is a product of production, not only with regard to the content, for only the results of production can be distributed, but also with regard to the form, since the particular mode of men's participation in production determines the specific form of distribution, the form in which they share in distribution." [2]

In every mode of social production, there are the means of subsistence and a surplus product to be distributed:

> Assuming some form of social production to exist (e.g., primitive Indian communities, or the more ingeniously developed communism of the Peruvians), a distinction can always be made between that portion of labor whose product is directly consumed individually by the producers and their families and—aside from the part which is productively consumed—that portion of labor which is invariably surplus-labor, whose product serves constantly to satisfy the general social needs, no matter how this surplus product may be divided, and no matter who may function as representative of these social needs.[3]

According to Marx, "capitalist distribution differs from those forms of distribution which arise from other modes of production." [4] Under capitalism, the means of subsistence accrue to labor in the form of wages—a payment for the commodity, labor power. The surplus product is distributed among capitalists, financiers, and landlords in the forms of profit, interest, and rent. "With the differences in distribution, *class differences* emerge." [5] The class structure of any society is thus determined by the mode of production. A change in the mode of production will cause a change in distribution and, thereby, a change in the class structure of society.

In the nineteenth century the view prevailed that society could effect any distribution of output it wished, independently of how it was produced. For example, consider John Stuart Mill's well-known statements: "The laws and conditions of the production of wealth partake of the character of physical truths," but "the distribution of wealth depends on laws and customs of society." [6] According to Engels, Dühring believed that "the capitalist mode of *production* is quite good, and can remain in existence, but the capitalist mode of *distribution* is bad and must disappear." [7] Marx spoke contemptuously of how "vulgar socialism . . . has taken over from the bourgeois economists the consideration and treatment of distribution as independent of the mode of production and hence the presentation of socialism as turning principally on distribution." [8] One of the principal differences between Marx's scientific socialism and what he called vulgar socialism is that Marx did not advocate reform of the commodity mode of production through redistribution, but its overthrow. Lenin referred to *The Critique of the Gotha Programme,* where Marx "contrasts vulgar socialism to scientific socialism, which attaches no great importance to distribution, explains the social system by the way the *relations of production* are organized, and considers that such organization already includes a definite system of distribution. This idea . . . runs through the whole of Marx's theory." [9]

Marx and Engels made only brief mention of distribution in a socialist mode of production. There would still be a surplus product, so that in effect each individual worker would be exploited by the community as a whole. Marx indicated that the surplus product would go for such things as general costs of administration, communal needs such as schools and health services, and funds for those unable to work.[10]

In the socialist mode of production, distribution to labor would not take the form of wages but would be effected through labor certificates that would not circulate as money. Since labor certificate schemes were suggested by a number of other nineteenth-century socialists and since Marx was critical of these schemes, it is necessary to show how Marx's concept of labor certificates differs from those of which he was critical.

Among some nineteenth-century socialists (Gray, Bray, Thompson, Hodgskin, Owen, and Rodbertus) a popular proposal was to substitute labor certificates for money. The use of certificates denominated in units of labor was supposed to eliminate the exploitation of labor, which they believed was caused by unequal exchange. They believed that exploitation results because the worker performs labor services of greater value than the payment he receives in exchange. They thought that this exploitation would be eliminated if instead of receiving payment in money, workers would receive payment in certificates that stated the number of hours of work performed. Such certificates would permit workers to acquire commodities equal in value to their labor services. Thus, they believed, there would be no surplus labor or exploitation. These socialist ideas inspired several unsuccessful attempts to establish labor exchange banks in England and France during the nineteenth century.*

Marx attacked these labor certificate schemes on the grounds that the proponents of them did not realize that the abolition of exchange was a precondition for the use of labor certificates. He thought that other socialists understood neither the nature of commodity production nor the nature of money. According to Marx, they did not understand the nature of money because they believed that "every commodity is immediately money." [11] "The idea of making sheep and vines attain the status of money is not new." [12] In effect, they wanted to transform labor into money by having labor acquire exchange value before it was exchanged.

But according to Marx the point is to eliminate money and exchange value altogether. In order to do this, it is necessary to eliminate commodity production. Marx criticized John Gray's labor certificate scheme because it was based on goods being *"produced as commodities but not exchanged as commodities."* He goes on to say:

> The fact that labor money is a pseudo-economic term, which denotes the pious wish to get rid of money, and together with money to get rid of exchange value, and with exchange value to get rid of commodities, and with commodities to get rid of the bourgeois mode of production—this fact, which remains concealed in Gray's work and of which Gray himself was not

---

* Engels refers to these Labor Exchange Bazaars in *Anti-Dühring*, (New York: International Publishers, 1967) p. 334n.

> aware, has been bluntly expressed by several British socialists, some of whom wrote earlier than Gray and others later.* But it was left to M. Proudhon and his school to declare seriously that the degradation of *money* and the exaltation of *commodities* was the essence of socialism and thereby to reduce socialism to an elementary misunderstanding of the inevitable correlation existing between commodities and money.[13]

For labor certificates to be used, exchange would have to be replaced by planned and directly associated labor. According to Marx, the labor certificate schemes of Bray and Owen would accomplish this, although neither of them realized it. With regard to Bray's scheme, Marx wrote: "Thus, if all the members of society are supposed to be actual workers, the exchange of equal quantities of hours of labor is possible only on condition that the number of hours to be spent on material production is agreed on beforehand. But such an agreement negates individual exchange."[14]

In a similar vein, Marx said of Owen's labor-money:

> I have elsewhere examined thoroughly the Utopian idea of "labor-money" in a society founded on the production of commodities. On this point I will only say further that Owen's "labor-money," for instance, is no more "money" than a

---

* Marx, in a footnote to this passage, mentioned John Bray and William Thompson. Contrary to Marx's assertion, neither Bray nor Thompson stated unambiguously that they wished to abolish exchange. For example, Thompson stated that he wanted to replace "forced" exchanges with "voluntary" exchanges. Thompson did indicate, however, that "voluntary" exchange included the relationship of mutual cooperation found in Robert Owen's utopian scheme. See William Thompson, *An Inquiry into the Principles of the Distribution of Wealth Most Conducive to Human Happiness* (New York: Augustus M. Kelley, 1963), p. 56n. Marx's terminology on this question is much clearer. Exchange refers to the relationship between mutually independent persons and does not refer to any relationship between directly associated persons.

> ticket for the theatre. Owen presupposes directly associated labor, a form of production that is entirely inconsistent with the production of commodities. The certificate of labor is merely evidence of the part taken by the individual in the common labor, and of his right to a certain portion of the common produce destined for consumption. But it never enters into Owen's head to presuppose the production of commodities, and at the same time, by juggling with money, to try to evade the necessary conditions of that production.[15]

Marx himself proposed the use of labor certificates as a tool in central planning. Marx differed from his socialist contemporaries in that he consciously incorporates these certificates as a part of planning.[16] According to Marx, only when society has consciously determined the social division of labor among different products so that all individual labor automatically becomes socially necessary labor will a labor certificate plan work. Marx's labor certificates are not money and would not circulate.*

Marx's scheme was not inspired by a wish to achieve equal exchanges. Society would have to receive a share of what is produced, so the labor certificate would not be equal in value to the socially necessary labor time performed.[17] Capitalist exploitation would be replaced with exploitation of the individual by society.

In *The State and Revolution,* Lenin paraphrased Marx when he wrote: "Every member of society, performing a certain part of the socially necessary work, receives a certificate from society to the effect that he has done a certain amount of work. And with this certificate he receives from the public store of consumer goods a corresponding quantity of prod-

* Since Marx connects the need for money with the existence of exchange, there is no need for money under socialism. In *The Critique of the Gotha Programme* Marx wrote that within the cooperative commonwealth based on the social ownership of the means of production, the producers do not exchange their products.

ucts. After a deduction is made of the amount of labor which goes to the public fund, every worker, therefore, receives from society as much as he had given to it." [18]

The ideas of Marx on labor certificate money, endorsed by Lenin, were the basis for the attempt by Soviet economists in 1921 to replace money by a labor unit of account called the "Tred."

— 6 —

Alienation and Historical Materialism

Perhaps no aspect of Marx has been more widely misinterpreted than his concept of alienation. Others who have found alienation to be a theme in Marx's writings have erred in explaining one result of commodity production, alienation, in terms of other results, greed or private property, or they have interpreted it from an "idealistic" standpoint* that is inconsistent with Marx's concept of historical materialism.[1] Their critics have correctly pointed out the incompatibility of "ideal-

* An "idealistic" concept of alienation is one that gives man's consciousness or psychology the role of a determinant. Marx referred to this view as a "fantasy," because it sees "the relationships of men, all their doings, their chains and their limitations [as] products of their consciousness." *The German Ideology* (New York: International Publishers, 1947), p. 6. According to Marx, this view suggests that man can change himself merely by exchanging one consciousness for another. To Marx, this view is foolish, because man's consciousness is determined by the mode of production: "the nature of individuals thus depends on the material conditions determining their production." *Ibid.*, p. 7.

istic" concepts of alienation with historical materialism,[2] but some erroneously concluded that a concept of alienation is not present in Marx's later writings. The discussion of Marxian alienation can be faulted for explaining one result in terms of other results, and for misunderstanding the issue of whether a concept of alienation is compatible with historical materialism.

Our interpretation [3] finds the source of Marxian alienation in exchange or the commodity mode of production, just as we have derived every other aspect of capitalism of which Marx was critical from commodity production. Marx's concept of alienation is materialistic—as it must be, given his materialist concept of history in which the institutions and consciousness of men (ideology in the classical Marxian sense) in any historical period are determined by the economic organization of society. In Marx's words: "The mode of production of material life conditions the general process of social, political, and intellectual life. It is not the consciousness of men that determines their existence, but their social existence that determines their consciousness." [4] Therefore greed is a derivative, not a determinant, in Marx's analysis of capitalism. Greed or money worship cannot then be the source of Marxian alienation; instead, it is a condition socialized into man by the ideological superstructure that results from the commodity mode of production.

There was no change in Marx's concept of the source of alienation from the *Manuscripts* in 1844 to *Capital* in 1867. In both works alienation is said to occur when men are mutually independent and engage in market exchange, and when men are subject to the market—something over which they have no control—as to an alien force. The lengthy discussion of the nature of commodities and the commodity mode of production in *Capital* is prefigured in the 1844 *Manuscripts*, in which Marx says that he has "considered the act of estranging practical human activity, labor, in two of its aspects. (1)

The relation of the worker to the *product of labor* as an alien object exercising power over him. . . . (2) The relation of labor to the *act of production* within the *labor* process."[5]

Marx says that in a capitalist economy "labor produces not only commodities: it produces itself and the worker as a *commodity*—and this in the same general proportion in which it produces commodities."[6] As a result, the worker "is looked upon as a supply of a *commodity* like any other. . . . his human qualities only exist insofar as they exist for capital *alien* to him." *

Marx is unequivocal in explaining that alienation is a consequence of the very act of production. The act of production is the act of producing commodities. Marx's criticism of economists has been generally misunderstood. It does not turn on drawing the implication of exploitation from the labor theory of value. Rather, Marx mainly criticizes economists for neglecting the organizational implications of commodity production. He says that *"political economy conceals the estrangement inherent in the nature of labor by not considering the direct relationship between the worker (labor) and production."*[7] Here Marx is saying that political economy conceals alienation by not considering that exchange separates production from use. All of Marx's economic writings from the *Manuscripts* through *Capital* have as their basis the examination of the relationship between the worker and the process of production. It is precisely this relationship which is the focus of Marx's analysis of alienation in the *Manuscripts*. He wrote:

---

* Marx, *The Economic and Philosophic Manuscripts of 1844* (New York: International Publishers, 1964), p. 120. Note that in the *Manuscripts* Marx refers to the worker as a commodity. He did not make the distinction between labor power which is a commodity and labor which is the use of labor power until later. In the *Grundrisse* he differentiated between the slave who is a commodity and the worker who sells his labor power as a commodity but is not himself a commodity. He retains this distinction in *Capital*.

> When we ask, then, what is the essential relationship of labor we are asking about the relationship of the *worker* to production.
>
> Till now we have been considering the estrangement, the alienation of the worker, only in one of its aspects, i.e., the worker's *relationship to the products of his labor*. But the estrangement is manifested not only in the result but in the *act of production,* within the producing activity, itself. How could the worker come to face the product of his activity as a stranger, were it not that in the very act of production he was estranging himself from himself? The product is after all but the summary of the activity of production. If then the product of labor is alienation, production itself must be active alienation, the alienation of activity, the activity of alienation. In the estrangement of the object of labor is merely summarized the estrangement, the alienation, in the activity of labor itself.[8]

In the *Manuscripts* Marx emphasizes that the dehumanizing of the worker occurs because of commodity production: "Production does not simply produce man as a *commodity,* the *human commodity,* man in the role of *commodity;* it produces him in keeping with this role as a *mentally* and physically *dehumanized* being.—Immorality, deformity, and dulling of the workers and the capitalists.—Its product is the *self-conscious* and *self-acting commodity* . . . the human commodity."[9]

It should be clearly understood that Marx's references to dehumanization and the plight of the individual do not mean that his concept of alienation is the same as the contemporary psychological and sociological concepts of it. Alienation of the sort Marx conceived cannot be treated by therapy for the worker and reform of the system; only a revolutionary change in the mode of production can overcome it. According to Marx, alienation is a consequence of objective economic conditions—the separation of production from use that characterizes the commodity mode of production. As Tucker has correctly observed, Marx "does not consider himself to be dealing with a psychiatric phenomenon. He regards himself as engaged in a criticism of political economy and believes that he has grasped and analyzed a fact of the economic life per se." [10] Marx states the relationship between alienation and economics several times in the *Manuscripts*. For example:

> It is hardly necessary to assure the reader conversant with political economy that my results have been attained by means of a wholly empirical analysis based on a conscientious critical study of political economy (p. 63). . . . We have proceeded from the premises of political economy (p. 106). . . . We took our departure from a fact of political economy—the estrangement of the worker and his production. We have formulated this fact in conceptual terms as *estranged, alienated* labor. We have analyzed this concept—hence analyzing merely a fact of political economy (p. 115). . . . political economy has merely formulated the laws of estranged labor (p. 117).

Some have argued that Marx jettisoned the concept of alienation after he had worked out the notion of historical materialism. Perhaps they have read an "idealistic" concept of alienation into Marx. It should be clear that Marx's concept of alienation is materialistic and as such is compatible with historical materialism. He did not drop the concept, but he found it difficult to use the term "alienation" because it had already established idealistic connotations among his socialist rivals and meant to many that man already possessed his true innate human nature to the full and was only prevented from enjoying it because of his bondage to religion or the capitalist.

In Marx, man's realization of his true human nature is a process of becoming. Man as a species has a true human nature, and it is innate in the possibilities of the species, although of course it is not innate in individual men in the stages of "prehistory." When communism arrives (the end of prehistory), mankind achieves the potential inherent in the species. The relations between men become (again) convivial (that is, there is directly associated production), and the relation of man to nature and to his own institutions is scientific. When Marx finds that man is alienated under commodity production, he is comparing him both to a past state and to a future one. In neither pre- nor post-capitalist systems is there a separation between production and use. Instead there is directly associated production with convivial relations between men and community control over economic life. Some have interpreted Marx's scheme in terms of fall and redemption. It is partially redemptive in that the convivial relations and community control over production which were destroyed by exchange are supposed to be restored under communism, but the basis for the directly associated production is different in pre- and post-capitalist systems. In a pre-capitalist system conviviality is rooted in community tradition and ritual; in the post-capitalist system it is rooted in a scientific consciousness. Since economic life controls human consciousness, society cannot have control over itself until it controls its economic life. Under capitalism, the control man gains over nature through technology is offset by the control his economic organization has over him.

Those who find in the *Manuscripts* a Marx different from the Marx of *Capital* have overlooked this paragraph from the *Manuscripts:* "Now, therefore, we have to grasp the essential connection between private property, greed, and the separation of labor, capital, and landed property; between exchange and competition, value and the devaluation of men, monopoly and competition, etc.—the connection between this whole estrangement and the *money* system." [11] Here in this concise paragraph Marx outlined his life work. In this book we have shown how Marx grasped the "essential connection" between these categories. He derives every aspect of capitalism from its mode of production. He does not derive one aspect of capitalism from one thing and another aspect from another thing. Neither does he proceed, as do many interpreters today, by deriving one aspect of capitalism from another; he does not explain one result in terms of another result. His uniformity of treatment of all aspects of capitalism is complete and does not exempt alienation. Let us now follow Marx's treatment of alienation from the 1844 *Manuscripts* through the *Critique of Political Economy* and *Capital*.

In the manuscript "Estranged Labor," Marx specifically denotes four aspects of man's alienation. First, there is the alienation of man from the product of his labor. The product of labor dominates man and not vice-versa. It has an existence independent of man as something alien to him and becomes a power that confronts him.

Second, man is alienated from labor itself—that is, from productive activity. Work becomes an activity that is external to, and independent of, the worker and an activity in which the worker finds no fulfillment. A worker does not produce use-value directly for himself or his community but exchange value for his employer. The external character of work for the worker is shown by the fact that it is not his own work but work for someone else, that in work he does not belong to himself but to another person.[12] The results of his own activity accrue to him only in his leisure; in what should be the most human of all activity—work—he is alienated.

The third aspect of alienated labor follows from the preceding two. Man is alienated from himself, his mental life, and his human life. Man's "life activity"—his labor—appears only as a means to satisfy his needs—that is, to make a living. But a man's work is his life; therefore, "life itself appears only as a *means to life*." [13]

Marx finds the fourth characteristic, that man is alienated from other men, to be a direct consequence of the other three. "What applies to a man's relation to his work, to the product of his labor, and to himself, also holds of a man's relation to the other man, and to the other man's labor and object of labor." [14]

In *A Contribution to the Critique of Political Economy*, Marx discusses the characteristics of labor that produces commodities. Labor that produces commodities is labor devoid of any quality. The individuality of labor is lost, and the specific forms of labor are lost because of their abstraction into money. Labor that produces commodities is labor that creates exchange value for the employer instead of use-value for the laborer. And, finally, labor that produces commodities "causes the social relations of individuals to appear in the perverted form of a social relation between things." [15]

Man is alienated from the objects of his labor, the work process, and from his own being when his labor loses its quality and individuality and when his labor is expended in producing for the market. Man is alienated from other men when his labor results in the personification of objects. Clearly, labor that creates commodities is alienated labor.

These characteristics of labor that produces commodities are revealed in the antitheses and contradictions which, in *Capital,* Marx finds to be inherent in commodities. In commodities are "the antithesis [between] use-value and [exchange] value; the contradiction that private labor is bound to manifest itself as direct social labor, that a particularized concrete kind of labor has to pass for abstract human labor; the contradiction between the personification of objects and the representation of persons by things." [16]

The various aspects of alienation given in the *Economic and Philosophic Manuscripts* are immanent in the nature of commodities. The contradictions and antitheses present in commodities, which are analyzed in *Capital,* are manifestations of alienation. The alienation of man from the product of his labor, from the work process itself, from his own being, and from other men is manifested in the contradictions between use-value and exchange value, individual labor and social labor, particular concrete labor and abstract general labor, and the personification of objects and representation of persons by things—all contradictions being inherent features of commodity production.

It is possible to pair single aspects of alienation with single contradictions immanent in a commodity. The alienation of man from his fellows is implied in "the personification of objects and the representation of persons by things."

The contradiction between use-value and exchange value implies the alienation of man from the objects of his own labor. Use-values follow from man producing directly for himself, his family, or his community; exchange values follow from man producing for the impersonal market through which the specific products of a man's work can serve other (unknown) men as use-values only after being exchanged.

The contradictions between individual labor and social labor and between specific concrete labor and abstract general labor imply the alienation of man from the work process. Marx says that labor which creates exchange value (commodities) is abstract general labor. From the viewpoint of the market it is immaterial who the individual worker is or whether he is a tailor or a carpenter. The specific concrete character of labor is lost by its abstraction into money.

The alienation of man from his own being follows from his alienation from the product of his labor and the work process. According to Marx, since man realizes himself in work, alienation from the products of his work and from productive activity results in alienation from his own being.

Alienation is immanent in Marx's concept of the two-fold character of labor embodied in commodities. In *Capital* he emphasized the importance he attached to this concept: "I was the first to point out and to examine critically this two-fold nature of the labor contained in commodities. As this point is the pivot on which a clear comprehension of Political Economy turns, we must go more into detail." [17] Labor that produces only use-values is not alienated labor but "a necessary condition, independent of all forms of society, for the existence of the human race." [18] Labor that produces commodities produces use-values only indirectly by producing exchange values. Exchange, which separates production from use, separates labor from the direct production of use-values.

Alienation begins when the purpose of production changes from direct use to exchange. In keeping with Marx's method, alienation is not a condition that engulfed man the moment the first commodities were produced. Just as the commodity mode of production evolved gradually, alienation evolved as exchange became predominant. Alienation became a general human condition with the appearance of labor markets in which men sell their labor power.

In capitalism, labor—man's human activity—cannot take place unless labor power is first sold in the market. Since man cannot even work unless he first sells his labor power, his loss of control over his life activity, the production process, himself as a laboring man, and his relations to other men, is total. This loss of control makes him powerless. If market conditions are such that labor power cannot be sold, then labor cannot be performed at all.

Marxian alienation is specific to systems in which exchange is predominant. This means that Marxian alienation characterizes the economies of the Soviet Union and East Europe. In these economies, labor power and the products of labor are commodities. If, as we believe, the natural structure of modern economy is polycentric,[19] exchange cannot be transcended, and Marxian alienation, if it is not a purely intellectual construction, is merely a fact of life.

One should not jump to the conclusions that by "alienation of man from the objects of his own labor" Marx is merely emphasizing exploitation of the worker and that by "alienation from the work process" Marx merely meant that the worker suffered under the monotony of the assembly line. It is clear in Marx that there can be exploitation without alienation, as in feudal exploitation.* Indeed, according to Marx, in *every* form of economy (including communism) men have a part of

* Exploitation is, as pointed out, the extraction of use-value beyond what is necessary to maintain and reproduce the worker and his family, whereas alienation is a consequence of exchange and is immanent in the *separation* of production from use.

their product expropriated. Marx does not treat surplus value as unique to capitalism. In the Asiatic, ancient, and feudal economies, there is a ruling class that lives by appropriating surplus value. Under communism, surplus value takes the form of use-value for the community: the individual is exploited by the community rather than by other individuals. Whereas exploitation is a characteristic of all economies, alienation is unique to capitalism because exchange as the predominant mode of production is unique to capitalism.

Having found alienation to be an inherent feature of commodity production, Marx proceeded to analyze the development of the capitalistic system. The contradictions and antitheses of that system, which Marx found revealed in such phenomena as crises, follow directly from the contradictions and antitheses immanent in commodity production, which in turn are manifestations of the various aspects of alienation. Although Marx made many references to the individual's plight, *Capital* is not a study of the psychological and sociological features of alienation. Marxian alienation is a feature of a particular mode of production, and it was the study of that mode of production which was the major work of Marx's life.

To summarize, we have shown that since labor which creates commodities is alienated labor, the contradictions in the relations of production of commodities reflect the characteristics of alienated labor. In the *Manuscripts,* Marx gives the characteristics of alienated labor. In the *Critique of Political Economy* and in *Capital,* he gives the characteristics of labor that produces commodities. We see that the characteristics of labor which produces commodities are the characteristics of alienated labor, and we conclude that commodities are produced by alienated labor. In *Capital,* Marx gives the contradictions inherent in the commodity mode of production. We see that these contradictions are manifestations of alienation, and we conclude that Marxian alienation is embodied in the phenomenon of commodity production.

This chapter has presented an interpretation of Marxian alienation that stands on its own. Nevertheless, some readers might ask how it fares when confronted with the prevalent interpretation that the division of labor is the source of alienation and is abolished under communism.[20] It is certainly true that Marx said that the specialization and division of labor within manufacture "converts the laborer into a crippled monstrosity, by forcing his detail dexterity at the expense of a world of productive capabilities and instincts"; [21] that "it is a result of the division of labor in manufactures that the laborer is brought face to face with the intellectual potencies of the material process of production, as the property of another, and as a ruling power"; [22] and that "some crippling of body and mind is inseparable even from division of labor in society as a whole. Since, however, manufacture carries this social separation of branches of labor much further, and also, by its peculiar division, attacks the individual at the very roots of his life, it is the first to afford the materials for, and to give a start to, industrial pathology." [23]

Our interpretation is not contradicted by this emphasis. What has misled others is their identification of the division of labor within the factory with the social division of labor and with the capitalist mode of production itself. However, Marx differentiates between (1) the division of labor within society (the social division of labor), (2) the division of labor within the factory, and (3) the mode of production upon which a social division of labor is established.

According to Marx, the division of labor in capitalist society "is brought about by the purchase and sale of the products of different branches of industry," [24] that is, by exchange. What then establishes "the connection between the detail operations in a workshop?" Marx says it comes about from "the sale of the labor power of several workmen to one capitalist, who applies it as combined labor power." [25] Marx ends his section in *Capital* on "Division of Labor in Manufacture and Division of Labor in Society" by saying perfectly clearly that, whereas a social division of labor is a characteristic of every economic formation of society, "division of labor in the workshop, as practiced by manufacture, is a special creation of the capitalist mode of production alone." [26] The crippling division of labor within the factory is then merely another result of the commodity mode of production, and not a determinant in Marx's system. It is production for market that produces the minute division of labor within the factory.

Marx, like Engels, contrasts the order within the firm with the anarchy of the organization between firms.[27] Once the social division of labor is established by a plan in an orderly way, like the division of labor within the firm, the anarchy of the market disappears along with exchange. When exchange is abolished, so is detail labor (the performance of "one and the same simple operation" by *a laborer all his life*). But neither the division of labor within society nor within the firm is abolished. Rather the effect of detailed labor on the individual is *evaded* by a social plan that rotates the work force through the various tasks.

In Marx's scheme there are really only three general social divisions of labor, each corresponding to a general mode of production. These are: (1) pre-capitalist production for direct use which has a social division of labor rooted in hereditary tradition (this general category contains Marx's specific historical forms of Asiatic, ancient, and feudal); (2) commodity production with a social division of labor established through market exchange; and (3) post-capitalist production for direct use in which a complex division of labor is not abolished but controlled by means of a social plan. Thus, the plan of the socialist or communist society is the mechanism for ending crises, alienation, the creation of private property through exchange, the individual's exploitation of individuals, and detail labor.

Marx sometimes uses the term "division of labor" in opposition to the organization of labor or the "directly associated labor" that characterizes the community which does not produce commodities; that is, he sometimes uses "division of labor" as a proxy for "mutually independent producers" or commodity production. Those who find division of labor to be the source of alienation perhaps have this use of the term in mind.

Others who have offered interpretations of Marxian alienation have found Marx to be a humanist.[28] Does our writing about Marxian alienation mean that we think Marx was a humanist?

We do not profess to know whether Marx was a humanist. Those who do claim to find a humanist in the young Marx of the 1844 *Manuscripts* would be on more solid ground if they gave some attention to the even younger Marx of 1843, who wrote that criticism "is a weapon. Its object is an *enemy* it wants not to refute but to *destroy*. . . . Criticism is no longer an *end in itself* but simply a *means*. Its essential pathos is *indignation,* its essential task, *denunciation*." Marx goes on to say that criticism is hand-to-hand combat, "and in such a combat the point is not whether the opponent is noble, equal, or interesting, the point is to *strike* him." [29]

Lenin would have found in these statements of the young Marx full support for the stand he took when charged by his own party with "conduct impermissible in a Party member." At his trial Lenin unflinchingly admitted that his choice of obnoxious phrases was "calculated to evoke in the reader hatred, aversion, and contempt . . . calculated not to convince but to break up the ranks of the opponent, not to correct the mistake of the opponent but to destroy him, to wipe his organization off the face of the earth. . . . Against such political enemies I then conducted . . . a fight of extermination." [30]

Those who find a humanist in Marx must also confront the remarkable account given by Hammen, which in effect portrays the young Marx as a good "Leninist" who selected the humanist vocabulary of the 1844 *Manuscripts* because it was in keeping with his "requirement that the revolutionary class be portrayed as representing the 'total loss of man,' with the victory of communism effecting the 'full recovery of man.' Concurrently, the existing bourgeois order had to be made to appear responsible for the enslavement, degradation, and estrangement of man."[31] Once a humanist vocabulary no longer suited his tactics, Marx abandoned it, and that is one reason why the 1844 *Manuscripts* were never published by Marx during his lifetime.

In our view, even if those who find the 1844 Marx a humanist can survive the 1843 Marx and Hammen's interpretation, they are still nowhere. The question does not turn on what sort of man Marx was, but on the programmatic implications of his work. That is why we ourselves have focussed not on Marx's personality but on the logic of his thought.

According to Marx, morality is only a mask for class interest. Thus, for Marxists, good will cannot be an effective force in history. Since each class acts in its own class interest, there is no humanistic basis upon which to unite classes and cultivate effective reforms. If there are as many specific moralities as there are class interests, what mediates between moralities? Marx answers that the mediator is violence. Lenin explicitly developed this doctrine of violence. According to Lenin, "the scientific concept of dictatorship means neither more nor less than unlimited power, resting directly on force, not limited by anything, not restricted by any laws, nor any absolute rules. Nothing else but that."[32]

Lenin's doctrine of violence was widely acknowledged by the Communist Party. For example, in 1928 Grigori Pyatakov, later a victim of the doctrine, recognized and approved it: "According to Lenin the Communist Party is based on the principle of coercion which doesn't recognize any limitations or inhibitions. And the central idea of this principle of boundless coercion is not coercion by itself but the absence of any limitation whatsoever—moral, political, and even physical."[33] Marx's reasoning, which leaves violence as the mediator between classes, leads logically to violence as the mediator between the Party and the people (Leninism), and even further to violence as the mediator between the Party and its members (Stalinism).

By showing that Stalinism is a logical derivation from the structure of Marx's writings, we do not mean to say that Marx was a Stalinist. Had Marx been in Stalin's historical position, he might have suspended his logic of violence in the interests of humanism, and perhaps Marx's view of communism has humanistic elements. The point is that Marx does not rely on humanism as the method by which to reach a humane communism. Indeed, parenthetical humanistic remarks notwithstanding, humane methods play no role in any part of Marx's account of historical change, neither in the transition from feudalism to capitalism nor in the transition from capitalism to communism. It is a strange humanist who does not rely on good will among men and humane methods of social change, but instead predicates violence as the force of history.

Eugene Kamenka, a Marxist philosopher who has published two studies on Marxism and ethics, begins one book by acknowledging:

> The rejection of any appeal to "abstract" moral principles was for many decades one of the best-known features of the work of Marx and Engels. Marxism was distinguished from utopian socialism precisely by reference to its *scientific* character, to its refusal to confront society with moral principles and moral appeals. "Communists preach no morality at all," Marx wrote (characteristically) in the *German Ideology* (1845–46). . . . Throughout the remainder of his life Marx would object bitterly to any attempt to base a socialist program on "abstract" moral demands embodied in such terms as "justice," "equality," etc.[34]

In his other study Kamenka states that "in the class society, the common interest is an illusion" and that "Marx's theory largely displaced and discredited" the "emphasis on the directing role of moral ideals." *

Engels, who is often superior to Marx in stating their common position clearly and simply, lets us see that whatever revision of Marx Lenin might have made, he did not revise the role of violence. Neither was Lenin the first to declare that good will does not exist as a basis for politics. Engels writes:

> Since the rising of class antagonism, the evil passions of men, greed, and imperiousness serve as the levers of historical progress, of which, for example, the history of feudalism and the bourgeoisie affords a conspicuous proof.[35]
>
> . . .
>
> Practical self-control with regard to ourselves and love, always love, in our intercourse with others are therefore the foundation rules of Feuerbach's morality, from which all others lead, and neither the enthusiastic periods of Feuerbach nor the loud praises of Starcke can set off the thinness and flatness of this pair of utterances.[36]

Engels says that the moral theories of Feuerbach are

> as powerless as Kant's "Categorical Imperative." As a matter of fact, every class, as well as every profession, has its own system of morals and breaks even this when it can do it without punishment. And love, which is to unite all, appears today in wars, controversies, lawsuits, domestic broils, and mutual plunder.[37]
>
> . . .
>
> But love, yes love, is particularly and eternally the magical god, who, according to Feuerbach, surmounts all the difficul-

---

* *The Ethical Foundations of Marxism* (London: Routledge and Kegan Paul, 1962), pp. 139, 143. Nevertheless, Kamenka seems to ascribe a "moral" tone to Marx. Perhaps it is the tone of "moral inversion." For this concept see Michael Polanyi, "Beyond Nihilism," in *Knowing and Being,* edited by Marjorie Grene (Chicago: University of Chicago Press, 1969).

> ties of practical life and that in a society which is divided into classes with diametrically opposing interests. The last remnant of its revolutionary character is thus taken from his philosophy, and there remains the old cant—'love one another.' [38]

The unbridled scorn that Engels pours on a "universal intoxication of reconciliation" is sufficient to have inspired Stalin's bloodiest thought and deed.

In the world today there are two distinct movements desperately struggling to revise Marxism into humanism. Neither movement has as its purpose the scholarly interpretation of Marx. The participants in both movements have as their purpose the use of Marx as a weapon against the social, economic, and political systems in which they live. In the communist lands of Eastern Europe and in the Soviet Union itself, "Marxian humanism" is fighting against the Communist Party of the Soviet Union to throw off the economic irrationality, cultural vacuity, totalitarianism, and terror of scientific Marxism. In communist lands "Marxian humanists" are fighting to erect humane sentiment and civic law as mediators between the rulers and the people.

In the nations of Western Europe and the Americas, "Marxian humanism" is a mask for, and a repackaging of, the old attacks against the traditional liberties and human feelings which "Marxian humanists" in communist lands are fighting to restore. Left-wing radicals and ideologues in the West find in the concept of alienation a subtler and more effective weapon against contemporary Western societies than the old Marxian slogans. The Polish philosopher and former Stalinist Leszek Kolakowski recently acknowledged the diametrical opposition of the two movements of "Marxian humanism":

> The Polish students who demonstrated in March 1968 were simply claiming the traditional liberties—freedom of speech, of press, of learning and assembly—which to some elements

> of the New Left are nothing but "treacherous bourgeois snares." A Polish friend of mine recently wrote to me from Sweden saying that whenever he had dealings with the New Left he seemed to be watching a film of which he already knew the end. That is exactly how I feel. The kind of language that was used in the past to justify the most brutal oppression is now being repeated as though nothing had ever happened.[39]

This book has given an exposition of Marx's analysis of capitalism and pointed out programmatic implications of that analysis. Marx's theory of exchange is one thing, but its programmatic implications are another. In the latter a utopian ideal of social perfection is embodied in a program of violence.

— 7 —

Summary

We have shown that there is a different perspective to Marx and have presented a view of him as an organizational theorist who found capitalism historically unique in terms of the purpose of its production. Production for exchange or the market gives capitalism a distinct form of social organization which Marx contrasted with pre- and post-capitalist modes of production. This is not to say that Marx saw no differences between socialism and Asiatic, ancient, and feudal modes of production—we have mentioned differences that he saw—but it is to say that he saw the purpose of all modes of production except capitalism to be production for direct use.

From these two different purposes of production follow two distinct organizational forms of society. In a capitalist or market society producers are mutually independent, and production is separated from consumption by exchange. The division of labor is determined by exchange, and this gives social organization a polycentric structure. It is unplanned and, according to Marx, anarchic. Unplanned production occurs because there are mutually independent producers. According to Marx, production for market cannot be planned; a planned market is a contradiction in terms. For Marx, production for the market necessarily separates value from price and brings on recurrent crises. It also creates alienation, because people are subjected to economic forces, forces of their own making, as to an external law.

In pre- and post-capitalist modes of production, men are not mutually independent but directly associated. In place of impersonal commercial relations, there are convivial relations of direct association. Direct association is hierarchic in structure. In pre-capitalist systems, the social division of labor was traditional and organized by status. Men were not equal, but they were not alienated. As a society, they had their own production under their own control. Although unequal, each man's production and consumption was consciously related to the community's production and consumption. Pre-capitalist society was subject to the external whims of nature but not to the whims of the market—productive relations of men's own making did not rule them as an external force. They were not subjected to the anarchy of the market.

In the post-capitalist system, direct association is to be organized by conscious planning. The hierarchic levels of planned production are the organizational expression of socialist conviviality and carry no social status: today a man is a manager, tomorrow an actor, the next day a farm worker. Although utopian, this follows logically in Marx's analysis.

Since the capitalist mode of production originates in exchange, all features of capitalism—commodities, capital, alienation, money, prices, detail labor, endless accumulation, rapid technological change, wages, intensification of exploitation, crises—have their origin in exchange. Private property is precisely capital and wages—both of which are products of exchange—and it is based on exchange rights.

Capitalism evolved from feudalism as a consequence of exchange permeating and breaking down the feudal community of directly associated producers. Exchange first took place between communities, but then penetrated the community itself, transforming the products of production, the means of production, and labor services into commodities. Marx described what Sir Henry Maine called the movement from status to contract in terms of the development of exchange.

The production of commodities results in the personification of objects which stand outside society and rule it as an external force. The prices of commodities "vary continually, independent of the will, foresight, and actions of the producers." [1] Just as prices vary continually, so do they diverge from value. When price falls below value, labor is wasted. Wasted or socially unnecessary labor means that the social division of labor is not correctly proportioned. Whenever the proportions of labor power allocated to the production of the various commodities are not correct, crises result. Thus, the reason for crises is disproportionality.

Marx's "law of value" is not a theory of price. Rather, it is a theory of how price fluctuations attempt to maintain correct labor proportions among the various industries. Although each individual producer plans his production, since the purpose of capitalist production is for the market, production for society as a whole is unplanned. This assures disproportionality. Thus, crises are an inherent characteristic of a society in which the social division of labor is established through market exchange.

Because of crises and the "anarchy of the market," Marx and Engels found bourgeois freedom to be illusory. For Marx and Engels, freedom comes with socialist planning, because planning removes society from subjugation to economic forces of its own making. The purpose of planning is to replace market exchange with production for direct use.*

* Since planning in the Soviet Union has failed to attain this aim, Soviet society is subject to autonomous economic forces of its own making. They stem from the contradictions of planning rather than from contradictions of the market, and the planning bureaucracy di-

Exchange is the cause of alienation just as it is the cause of crises. Planning cures both. Marx wrote that "with the communistic regulation of production (and, implicit in this, the destruction of the alien relation between men and what they themselves produce), the power of the relation of supply and demand is dissolved into nothing and men get . . . production . . . under their own control again." [2]

When we considered possible alternative sources of alienation—private property, greed, division of labor, exploitation—we found the arguments faulty either for explaining one result of exchange in terms of another result, or for explaining alienation in terms of phenomena that are not unique to capitalism (whereas alienation is).

We have shown that Marx's concept of alienation is materialistic and compatible with historical materialism. The Marx of the *Manuscripts* and the Marx of *Capital* are the same Marx with the same concept of alienation.

It is incorrect to assume, however, that because Marx's work contains a concept of alienation he was a humanist. Marx's concept of alienation does not imply humanism. Furthermore, his concept of violence as the mediator between different interests and as the force of history implies Leninism and Stalinism. It rules out a humanist reliance on good will among men as a vehicle for social change. Marx's concept of alienation serves as a weapon in his battle against capitalism; it is used in keeping with his dictum that criticism is a weapon whose object is to destroy an enemy. In Marx's scheme, alienation is not overcome until capitalism is destroyed and planned production for direct use takes the place of production for the market. When exchange ceases, so does alienation. Private property (wages and capital), detail labor, money, exchange value, crises, and commodities also disappear. Division of labor remains a feature of society, but it is planned,

---

rects its attention primarily to overcoming problems created by its own existence. See Roberts, *Alienation and the Soviet Economy* (Albuquerque: University of New Mexico Press, 1971).

and labor is directly associated. Work (the expenditure of human labor) and exploitation also remain, but the purpose of production no longer fosters the accumulation of surplus value as an end in itself. Surplus labor is appropriated for social (not individual) use.

Marx was not principally concerned with drawing the implication of exploitation from the labor theory of value. Marxian socialism is not achieved by public ownership of property and a more equal distribution of income and wealth. Marx was contemptuous of "vulgar socialism" founded on these principles. Such socialism was not scientific because it sought to reform capitalism and did not strike at the heart of that system—exchange. Indeed, according to Marx, other socialists did not fully understand the fundamental nature of capitalism.

Public ownership of property is not the defining characteristic of Marxian socialism; central planning is. In Marxian socialism, there is no exchange; therefore, there is no private property (rights to exchange). There are only use-rights, so "ownership" of property would not mean the same thing as it does in capitalism. Elimination of exchange rights eliminates private property in capital and in labor services. The worker would not exchange his ownership of labor time for wages. He would receive the means of subsistence by redemption of labor certificates, which would be requisitons to society's stock room of use-values.

Marx did not advocate the redistribution of income within a system of commodity production. He did not view national income as a pie that could be distributed independently of the way it was produced. He saw income distribution in a market system as determined by what one could get in exchange. He did not advocate the reform of commodity production; he advocated its overthrow.

From our emphasis on the central role of exchange in Marx's theory of capitalism, we hope others will find that muddy Marxian streams now run clearer.

Appendix

Marxian Crises As Market Disequilibrium

In Chapter Four it was shown that Marx treats crises as consequences of market disproportionality. Disproportionality means that there is a misallocation of resources among some or all industries, so that supply and demand for the products of these industries are not equal at prevailing market prices. In other words, disproportionality means that markets are in disequilibrium.

The purpose of this Appendix is to demonstrate that there is a close similarity between Marx's analysis of markets in disequilibrium—that is, Marx's analysis of crises—and the analyses of market disequilibrium by Clower, Leijonhufvud, Grossman and Barro.[1] Marx's analysis of crises has more in common with modern analysis of market disequilibrium than it does with the analysis of business cycles advanced by the Keynesians.* Attempts to put Marx's analysis of crises into a

* Marx's analysis is similar to that which Leijonhufvud attributes to Keynes but not to the Keynesians. We are not concerned here with

Keynesian framework are forced and lack foundation in Marx's writings.[2]

We do not deny that there is similarity between Marx's analysis and the Keynesian one. Both reject Say's Law of Markets.[3] Marx attacked Ricardo's statement of Say's Law that "productions are always bought by productions, or by services; money is only the medium by which the exchange is effected." [4] According to Marx, Say's Law assumes away the existence of commodity production, and thus it assumes away the possibility of crises. Marx stated that

> the *commodity,* in which the antagonism between exchange value and use-value exists, is transformed [by the assumptions of Say's Law] into a simple product (use-value), and consequently the exchange of commodities is transformed into a mere bartering of products, of simple use-values. This is to go back not only to before capitalist production, but to before simple commodity production; and the most developed phenomenon of capitalist production—world market crises—is flatly denied by the flat denial of the first condition of capitalist production, namely, that the product is a commodity and must therefore take the form of money and pass through the process of metamorphosis. . . . Inasmuch as, through the transformation of the commodity into mere use-value (product), the essence of exchange value is expunged, it is then easy to deny—or rather it is necessary to deny—*money* as an essential and independent form of the commodity in the process of the metamorphosis from its original form. In this way, therefore, crises are reasoned out of existence through losing sight of or denying the first pre-conditions of capitalist production: the nature of the product as a commodity, the duplication of the commodity in commodity and money, the consequent separate phases in the exchange of commodities, and finally the relation of money or commodities to wage labor.[5]

---

the dispute about whether there is a difference between Keynes and the Keynesians. To avoid confusion, however, we shall say that Marx's analysis is contrary to that of the Keynesians as this group is defined by Leijonhufvud.

Say's Law allows for partial overproduction but not for general overproduction. If there is excess supply of one commodity, there is excess demand for another, but there cannot be an excess supply of all commodities (a general glut). In contrast, Marx argued that partial overproduction may lead to general overproduction. He reasoned that if a particular commodity could not be sold for money, then it is possible that all commodities or a portion of all commodities could not be sold for money. Marx wrote: "At a given moment the supply of all commodities may be greater than the demand for all commodities, because the demand for the general commodity, money, exchange value, is greater than the demand for all particular commodities; in other words, because the compulsion for the commodity to take the form of money, to realize its exchange value, is greater than the compulsion for the commodity to be converted into use-value." [6]

This quotation approximates Walras' Law: the aggregate value of the excess supplies of commodities is always equal to the excess demand for money. In symbolic form, Walras' Law is:

$$X \equiv p_1S_1 + p_2S_2 + \ . \ . \ . \ + p_nS_n,$$

where $p_1, p_2, \ldots, p_n$ represent the prices of n goods, $S_1, S_2, \ldots S_n$ represent their excess supplies, and X represents the excess demand for money. The excess supplies and excess demand for money can be positive, negative, or zero.[7] The identity indicates that excess supplies of commodities and the excess demand for money are non-zero only at certain prices. It is evident that Marx understood the relationship between excess supplies, excess demands, and prices when he said that "the excess of commodities is always relative, that is, it is an excess at certain prices." [8]

Walras wanted to demonstrate the theoretical possibility of a set of prices for which the excess supply of each commodity and the excess demand for money are zero. This set of prices is found by the process of *tâtonnement*—an auctioneer calls out a set of prices to which traders respond by indicating on tickets the amounts they would buy or sell. If, however, that set of prices does not clear all markets so that excess supplies and demands are zero everywhere, then no transactions take place and a new set of prices is called out. This process of "groping" continues until a set of prices is found for which all markets are in equilibrium—there are no excess supplies or demands. By this method, Walras was able to demonstrate the theoretical possibility of general equilibrium.

Marx was not interested in showing the theoretical possibility of general equilibrium. He wanted to show instead the probability of general disequilibrium. In Marx's analysis of markets, there is no auctioneer or "recontracting"—Edgeworth's method of arriving at a set of market-clearing prices. In Marx, transactions take place at prevailing market prices regardless of excess supplies or demands. A crisis is the process by which equilibrium in markets is restored. "Crisis is nothing but the forcible assertion of the unity of phases of the production process which have become independent of each other." [9] Thus, in effect, crises perform the same function (the achievement of an equilibrium) in Marx's analysis that is performed in Walras' analysis by the auctioneer. The difference, of course, is that in Marx the market equilibrium is achieved only after values are destroyed, resources are unemployed (at least temporarily), and unsold products are wasted.

The principal point of similarity between Marx's analysis of crises and models of market disequilibrium is that both emphasize the effects of the constraint imposed on the ability to buy in other markets by the failure to sell in one market. This constraint is evident in each of the two ways in which Marx saw the general possibility of crises. The possibility of crises exists (1) because "money functions as a *means of circulation,* through the separation of purchase and sale," and (2) because "it functions as a *means of payment,* where it has two separate aspects, as *measure of value* and as *realization of value.*" [10]

According to Marx, the separation of purchase and sale means that purchases are constrained by sales. This constraint appears in Marx's model of the simple circulation of commodities, C-M-C, where the Cs are commodities and M is money. The process, C-M-C, is divided into two stages, sale or C-M, and purchase or M-C.[11] A person cannot buy commodities, M-C, unless he has first sold commodities, C-M.

The simple circulation of commodities is characteristic of the pre-capitalist stage of the commodity mode of production. However, it is important to remember that C-M-C takes place as a necessary counterpart to the process of capital circulation, M-C-M. Marx expanded this short form of the circulation of capital into a more detailed form M-C . . . P . . . C′-M′, where M-C represents the purchase of labor power, P represents the production process and the dots indicate that the process of circulation is interrupted, and C′-M′ represents the sale of commodities that have been produced.[12] The process of capital circulation is continuous; so the capitalist uses M′ to purchase more labor power. The end of one circulation, the sale of the product, C′-M′, becomes the beginning of a new circulation with the purchase of labor power, M′-C. Thus in the process of capital circulation there exists the simple circulation of commodities, C′-M′-C. With this formulation, it can be seen that the capitalist's ability to buy labor power, M′-C, is constrained by his ability to sell his product, C′-M′. If he cannot sell or can sell only at prices below value, a crisis results. Marx wrote:

> The general possibility of crises which is contained in this form—the separation of purchase and sale [C-M-C]—is therefore implicit in the movement of capital, in so far as this capital is *also* commodity and nothing but commodity. . . . Consequently, the separation of purchase from sale appears here also in such a way that the transformation of one capital from the form commodity into the form money must correspond to the re-transformation of the other capital from the form money into the form commodity. . . . This mutual confluence and intertwining of the reproduction or circulation processes of different capitals is . . . accidental.[13]

The capitalist is constrained from buying labor power by his inability to sell his output or his ability to sell it only at prices below value. This means that workers are unable to sell their labor power or can sell it only at lower wages. Simple circulation of commodities, C-M-C, prevails among workers who sell their labor power, C-M, in order to buy commodities for consumption, M-C. The inability of the workers to sell their labor power constrains their ability to buy commodities. Marx wrote:

> If therefore through any circumstance whatever or a combination of circumstances the market price of the commodities (of all or of the majority—it makes no difference) falls far below their price of production [or value], then, in the first place, the reproduction of capital will be considerably curtailed. Even more, however, will accumulation be held back. . . . The check in reproduction leads to a decrease of variable capital, to a fall in wages and a fall in the amount of labor employed. This in turn reacts anew on prices and brings about a new fall in prices.[14]

Excess supply in commodity markets and excess supply in labor markets are mutually reinforcing. Capitalists want labor power but lack the means of payment because they did not sell some of their output. Workers want commodities but do not have the means of payment because of unemployment and a decrease in wages. In a crisis, unemployed workers with unfilled wants exist side by side with unsold and seemingly overproduced commodities. Use-values have been produced but they cannot fulfill needs. Marx indicated that overproduction has nothing to do with absolute needs. "It is only needs with capacity to pay that count." [15]

The constraint imposed by disequilibrium in one market on other markets is evident in Marx's discussion of the second reason for the possibility of crises—the fact that when money serves as a means of payment it has two separate aspects, a measure of value and a realization of value. As a measure of value, money indicates what the seller, the capitalist, plans to receive from the sale of commodities. Marx says that money in this aspect is "ideal" or "imaginary" money.[16] To use Clower's term, it may be called "notional" money.[17] It is the money measure of the labor embodied in the product which the capitalist assumes to be socially necessary labor, that is, labor expended on products for which he assumes there is a demand. Before products are sold supply is a planned or notional supply.

Money, in its role as a realization of value (standard of price), indicates the amount actually received when commodities are sold. It is at that moment the capitalist finds out what the demand in the market actually is. This is the "effective" demand for commodities. When Marx writes that "production without regard to the limits of the market is therefore in the nature of capitalist production," [18] he means that production is necessarily based on planned revenue (money as a measure of value), and not on actual revenue (money as a realization of value).

In market disequilibrium models, the existence of excess supply at prevailing prices in any one market makes effective demand fall short of notional demand in other markets.[19] The constraint on the income of sellers in any market experiencing excess supply serves as a constraint on sales and the income of sellers in other markets. In Marx's analysis, if money as a measure of value is greater than money as realization of value, a crisis results. In effect, capitalists have misjudged the extent of the market and some goods are unsold. We are back to Marx's explanation of the first possibility of crises. Unsold goods in one market serve as a constraint on purchases in other markets. Marx supposes a disequilibrium in the market for cotton goods and he describes the consequences as follows:

> The stagnation in the market, which is over-supplied with cottons, disturbs reproduction for the weaver. This distur-

bance first affects his workers. The latter therefore are now to a smaller extent, or not at all, consumers of his commodity —cotton—and of other commodities which enter into their consumption. They have, it is true, a need for cottons, but they cannot buy them because they have not the means to do so, and they have not the means because they cannot continue to produce, and they cannot continue to produce because too much has been produced, too many cotton goods are in store on the market. . . . They now constitute a part of the temporary overproduction, overproduction of workers, in this case of cotton producers, because there is an overproduction of cotton goods on the market.

But apart from the workers employed directly by the capital invested in cotton weaving, numbers of other producers are affected by this check in the reproduction of cotton: spinners, cotton growers, producers of spindles and looms, of iron, coal, and so on. All these would be similarly checked in their reproduction, as the reproduction of cotton goods is the condition for their own reproduction. This would take place, even if they had not over-produced in their own spheres, that is, had not produced beyond the limit set by and justified by the cotton industry when it was going swimmingly. All these industries have only this in common: that they consume their revenue (wages and profit, in so far as the latter is consumed as revenue and not accumulated) not in the form of their own product, but in the product of the spheres which produce articles of consumption, of which cotton is one. So the consumption and the demand for cotton falls, precisely because there is too much of it on the market. But so also does that of all other commodities on which, as articles of consumption, the revenue of these indirect producers of cotton cloth is spent. The means with which they can buy cotton cloth and other articles of consumption become restricted and contract, because there is too much cotton on the market. This affects also other commodities (articles of consumption). They are now suddenly in *relative* overproduction, because the means to buy them, and therewith the demand for them, have contracted. Even if there has been no overproduction in these spheres, now they are overproducing.[20]

According to Marx, economic crisis, which is inherent in the separation of production from use, can be set off by such things as a technological change,[21] bad harvests because of weather conditions,[22] or simply miscalculation because the capitalist seeks not to reproduce his capital but to expand it by accumulation.[23] If the disequilibrium (overproduction) occurs in the market for "leading articles of commerce," then other markets are more likely to be thrown out of equilibrium.[24] If this occurs, disequilibrium affects all markets and there is a general glut of commodities.

Paul Sweezy argues that the problem of crises does not receive a complete or systematic treatment in Marx's writings.[25] Our interpretation of Marx's writings suggests that crises mean that markets are in disequilibrium. If this is correct, Marx's analysis of crises may not be systematic or elegant, but it is complete.

Notes

PREFACE

1. Paul A. Samuelson, "Wages and Interest: A Modern Dissection of Marxian Economic Models," *American Economic Review*, December 1957, p. 911.

2. Paul M. Sweezy, *The Theory of Capitalist Development* (New York: Monthly Review Press, 1942).

3. Frank Knight, "The Role of Principles in Economics and Politics," *American Economic Review*, March 1951, pp. 1–29. James M. Buchanan, "What Should Economists Do?" *Southern Economic Journal*, January 1964, pp. 213–22. Kenneth Boulding, "The Relations of Economic, Political, and Social Systems," in *Beyond Economics* (Ann Arbor: University of Michigan Press, 1968), pp. 98–112.

4. See Oscar J. Hammen, "Alienation, Communism, and Revolution in the Marx-Engels Breifwechsel," *Journal of the History of Ideas*, Vol. XXXIII, No. 1 (January–March 1972), and "The Young Marx Reconsidered," *Journal of the History of Ideas*, Vol. XXXI, No. 1 (January–March 1970).

5. Thomas Sowell, "Marx's *Capital* After One Hundred Years," *Canadian Journal of Economics and Political Science*, February 1967.

1: MARX AS AN ORGANIZATIONAL THEORIST

1. Karl Marx, *Capital* I (New York: International Publishers, 1967), p. 235.

2: THE COMMODITY MODE OF PRODUCTION

1. Karl Marx, *Capital* I (New York: International Publishers, 1967), p. 82.

2. Frederick Engels, *Anti-Dühring* (New York: International Publishers, 1939), p. 334.

3. Marx, *Capital* I, p. 72.

4. *Ibid.*, p. 114.

5. *Ibid.*, p. 39.

6. *Ibid.*, p. 36.

7. *Ibid.*, p. 40.

8. *Ibid.*, pp. 41, 42.

9. *Ibid.*, p. 37.

10. *Ibid.*, p. 38.

11. *Ibid.*

12. *Ibid.*, p. 44.

13. *Ibid.*, p. 75.

14. *Ibid.*, p. 81.

15. Karl Marx, *Capital* III (New York: International Publishers, 1967), p. 831.

16. Marx, *Capital* I, p. 621.

17. Marx, *Capital* III, pp. 879–80.

18. Marx, *Capital* I, p. 359.

19. *Ibid.*, p. 430.

20. *Ibid.*, p. 353.

21. *Ibid.*, p. 351.

22. *Ibid.*, p. 87.

23. Engels, *Anti-Dühring*, p. 339.

24. Marx, *Capital* I, p. 168.

25. Karl Marx, *A Contribution to the Critique of Political Economy* (New York: International Publishers, 1970), p. 36.

26. Marx, *Capital* I, p. 352.

27. *Ibid.*

28. See, for example, Kenneth Boulding, "The Relations of Economic, Political, and Social Systems," in *Beyond Economics* (Ann Arbor: University of Michigan Press, 1968).

29. Marx, *Capital* I, p. 42.

30. *Ibid.*, pp. 354–55.

31. *Ibid.*, pp. 40–41.

32. Karl Marx, *Pre-Capitalist Economic Formations* (New York: International Publishers, 1965), p. 96.

33. *Ibid.*, p. 111.

34. Marx, *Critique of Political Economy*, p. 22.

35. Frederick Engels, "Outlines of a Critique of Political Economy," reprinted in Karl Marx, *The Economic & Philosophic Manuscripts of 1844* (New York: International Publishers, 1964), p. 206.

36. Marx, *Economic and Philosophic Manuscripts*, p. 162.

37. Karl Marx, *The Poverty of Philosophy* (New York: International Publishers, 1963), p. 81.

38. Marx, *Pre-Capitalist Economic Formations*, p. 115.

39. Frederick Engels, *The Origin of the Family, Private Property, and the State* (New York: International Publishers, 1942), p. 101.

40. Marx, *Capital* I, p. 715.

41. Marx, *Critique of Political Economy*, p. 34.

42. Marx, *Pre-Capitalist Economic Formations*, p. 83.

43. Marx, *Critique of Political Economy*, p. 208.

44. Marx, *Capital* I, p. 718.

45. *Ibid.*

46. *Ibid.*, p. 723.

47. *Ibid.*, p. 715.

48. Marx, *Capital* III, pp. 790–802.

49. *Ibid.*, p. 798.

50. *Ibid.*, p. 802.

51. Marx, *Pre-Capitalist Economic Formations*, p. 95.

52. Marx, *Economic and Philosophic Manuscripts*, p. 117.

53. Marx, *Capital* I, p. 763.

54. Marx, *Pre-Capitalist Economic Formations*, pp. 113–14.

55. Marx, *Capital* I, p. 761.

56. *Ibid.*, p. 77.

57. *Ibid.*

58. *Ibid.*, pp. 77–78.

59. Marx, *Capital* III, p. 882.

60. Karl Marx, *The German Ideology* (New York: International Publishers, 1947), p. 24.

61. *Ibid.*, pp. 25–26.

62. Marx, *Capital* I, p. 80.

63. Engels, *Anti-Dühring*, p. 307.

64. *Ibid.*, p. 309.

65. Paul Craig Roberts, *Alienation and the Soviet Economy* (Albuquerque: University of New Mexico Press, 1971), Ch. 6.

66. Marx, *The German Ideology*, p. 77.
67. Engels, *Anti-Dühring*, p. 310.
68. *Ibid.*, p. 125.
69. Marx, *The German Ideology*, p. 22.
70. Marx, *Economic and Philosophic Manuscripts*, p. 118.
71. Engels, *Anti-Dühring*, p. 299.
72. *Ibid.*, p. 309.
73. V. I. Lenin, *State and Revolution* (New York: Little Lenin Library, 1932), p. 84.
74. Marx, *The German Ideology*, p. 22.

3: CAPITAL

1. Karl Marx, *Capital* I (New York: International Publishers, 1967), p. 233.
2. Karl Marx, *The Economic and Philosophic Manuscripts of 1844* (New York: International Publishers, 1964), p. 78.
3. Marx, *Capital* I, p. 209.
4. *Ibid.*
5. *Ibid.*, p. 153.
6. Karl Marx, *Pre-Capitalist Economic Formations* (New York: International Publishers, 1965), p. 119.
7. Karl Marx, *The Poverty of Philosophy* (New York: International Publishers, 1963), p. 185.
8. Eugen von Bohm-Bawerk, *Positive Theory of Capital*, Volume II of *Capital and Interest*, trans. George D. Huncke and Hans F. Sennholz (South Holland, Illinois: Libertarian Press, 1959), pp. 10–15.
9. Marx, *Pre-Capitalist Economic Formations*, p. 120.
10. *Ibid.*, p. 118.
11. Marx, *Capital* I, p. 170.
12. Marx, *Pre-Capitalist Economic Formations*, p. 105.
13. *Ibid.*, p. 107.
14. Marx, *Capital* I, p. 146.
15. Marx, *Pre-Capitalist Economic Formations*, p. 112.
16. Frederick Engels, *Anti-Dühring* (New York: International Publishers, 1939), p. 339.
17. Marx, *Pre-Capitalist Economic Formations*, p. 110.
18. *Ibid.*, p. 111.
19. *Ibid.*, pp. 105–6.

20. Karl Marx, *The German Ideology* (New York: International Publishers, 1947), p. 44.

21. Marx, *Capital* I, pp. 742–44.

22. Marx, *Pre-Capitalist Economic Formations*, p. 108.

23. *Ibid.*, p. 118.

24. Marx, *Capital* I, p. 595.

25. *Ibid.*, pp. 152–53.

26. *Ibid.*, pp. 151–52.

27. *Ibid.*, p. 152.

28. *Ibid.*, p. 589.

29. *Ibid.*, p. 152 n.1.

30. *Ibid.*, p. 184.

31. Marx, *The German Ideology*, p. 52.

32. William Thompson, *An Inquiry into the Principles of The Distribution of Wealth Most Conducive to Human Happiness* (New York: Augustus M. Kelley, 1963), pp. 45–67. John F. Bray, *Labour's Wrongs and Labour's Remedy or The Age of Might and the Age of Right* (New York: Augustus M. Kelley, 1968), pp. 48–52.

33. Marx, *Capital* I, p. 176.

34. *Ibid.*, p. 235.

35. *Ibid.*, p. 77.

36. *Ibid.*

37. *Ibid.*, pp. 231–35.

38. Marx, *The Poverty of Philosophy*, p. 109.

39. Marx and Engels, *Manifesto of the Communist Party*, in *Selected Works* (Moscow: Foreign Languages Publishing House, 1958), p. 37.

4: VALUE AND CRISES

1. Karl Marx, *The Economic and Philosophic Manuscripts of 1844* (New York: International Publishers, 1964), p. 72.

2. *Ibid.*, pp. 88–89.

3. *Ibid.*, p. 90.

4. Frederick Engels, "Outlines of a Critique of Political Economy," reprinted in Marx, *Economic and Philosophic Manuscripts*, pp. 214–15.

5. *Ibid.*, p. 215.

6. Karl Marx, *The Poverty of Philosophy* (New York: International Publishers, 1963), p. 68.

7. *Ibid.*

8. *Ibid.*, p. 69.

9. *Ibid.*, p. 68.

10. Karl Marx, *Capital* I (New York: International Publishers, 1967), p. 114.

11. Engels, "Outlines of a Critique of Political Economy," p. 214.

12. Marx, *Capital* I, p. 356.

13. *Ibid.*, pp. 354–55. See also Karl Marx, *Capital* III (New York: International Publishers, 1967), pp. 635–36.

14. Marx, *Capital* III, p. 635.

15. *Ibid.*, p. 188.

16. *Ibid.*, p. 187. See also Marx, *Capital* I, pp. 106–7.

17. Marx, *Capital* III, p. 117.

18. *Ibid.*, pp. 254–56.

19. *Ibid.*, p. 257.

20. Frederick Engels, *Anti-Dühring* (New York: International Publishers, 1939), p. 340.

21. *Ibid.*, pp. 337–38.

22. Marx, *The Poverty of Philosophy*, p. 69.

23. See, for example, Paul A. Samuelson, "Understanding the Marxian Notion of Exploitation: A Summary of the So-Called Transformation Problem Between Marxian Values and Competitive Prices," *Journal of Economic Literature*, IX, No. 1 (June 1971), pp. 399–431.

24. Marx, *Capital* III, p. 179.

25. Karl Marx, *A Contribution to the Critique of Political Economy* (New York: International Publishers, 1970), p. 96.

26. *Ibid.*, p. 48.

27. Marx, *Capital* I, p. 97.

28. *Ibid.*, pp. 101–2.

29. *Ibid.*, p. 101.

30. *Ibid.*, p. 94 n. 1.

31. Marx, *The Poverty of Philosophy*, p. 87.

32. *Ibid.*, p. 88.

33. Marx, *Capital* I, p. 102.

34. *Ibid.*, pp. 113–14.

35. *Ibid.*, pp. 106–7.

36. *Ibid.*, p. 139.

37. *Ibid.*, p. 137.

38. *Ibid.*, p. 139.

39. Marx, *Capital* III, p. 254.

40. Karl Marx, *Capital* II (New York: International Publishers, 1967), p. 75.

41. *Ibid.*, p. 76.

42. *Ibid.*, pp. 410–11.

43. Marx, *Capital* III, p. 258.

5: DISTRIBUTION

1. Karl Marx, *Capital* III (New York: International Publishers, 1967), p. 882. Cf. Engels, *Anti-Dühring* (New York: International Publishers, 1938), pp. 164, 170, 326.

2. This manuscript, "Introduction," is included in the Appendices to Karl Marx, *A Contribution to the Critique of Political Economy* (New York: International Publishers, 1970). The quotation is from p. 200.

3. Marx, *Capital* III, pp. 877–78.

4. *Ibid.*, p. 883.

5. Engels, *Anti-Dühring*, p. 165.

6. John Stuart Mill, *Principles of Political Economy with Some of Their Applications to Social Philosophy* (London: 1923), pp. 199–200.

7. Engels, *Anti-Dühring*, p. 326.

8. Marx, *Critique of the Gotha Programme* (New York: International Publishers, 1938), p. 11.

9. V. I. Lenin, *The Economic Content of Narodism and the Criticism of It in Mr. Struve's Book*, in *Collected Works* (Moscow: Foreign Languages Publishing House, 1960), Vol. 1, p. 442.

10. Marx, *Critique of the Gotha Programme*, p. 7.

11. Marx, *Critique of Political Economy*, p. 85.

12. Marx, *The Poverty of Philosophy* (New York: International Publishers, 1963), p. 89.

13. Marx, *Critique of Political Economy*, p. 86.

14. Marx, *Poverty of Philosophy*, p. 77.

15. Marx, *Capital* I (New York: International Publishers, 1967), p. 94 n. 1.

16. *Ibid.*, pp. 78–79.

17. Marx, *Critique of the Gotha Programme*, p. 8.

18. V. I. Lenin, *The State and Revolution*, in *Collected Works* (Moscow: Progress Publishers, 1964), Vol. 25, p. 465.

6: ALIENATION AND HISTORICAL MATERIALISM

1. Daniel Bell, for example, finds the source of alienation in private property and the division of labor, with exploitation and dehumanization being the features of alienation. Robert Tucker, for example, finds the source of alienation in greed. In a later work, Tucker finds the source of alienation in the division of labor. See Bell, "The Debate on Alienation," in *Revisionism: Essays on the History of Marxist Ideas,* edited by Leopold Labedz (New York: Praeger, 1962). See Tucker, *Philosophy and Myth in Karl Marx* (Cambridge: Cambridge University Press, 1961), and *The Marxian Revolutionary Idea* (New York: Norton, 1969). Unlike Tucker, Bell does not find alienation to be a concern of the mature Marx. See Bell, *The End of Ideology* (Glencoe: The Free Press, 1960), p. 344.

2. See Sidney Hook, *From Hegel to Marx: Studies in the Intellectual Development of Karl Marx* (Ann Arbor: University of Michigan Press, 2nd ed. 1962), and "Marxism in the Western World: From 'Scientific Socialism' to Mythology," in *Marxist Ideology in the Contemporary World,* edited by M. Drachkovitch (New York: Praeger, 1966). See also Hook, *Slavic Review,* Vol. XXI, pp. 552–53 and Vol. XXII, pp. 189–90.

3. See P. C. Roberts and M. A. Stephenson, "Alienation and Central Planning in Marx," *Slavic Review,* Vol. XXVII, No. 3 (September 1968); "A Note on Marxian Alienation," *Oxford Economic Papers,* Vol. 22, No. 3 (November 1970); and P. C. Roberts, *Alienation and the Soviet Economy* (Albuquerque: University of New Mexico Press, 1971).

4. Karl Marx, *A Contribution to the Critique of Political Economy* (New York: International Publishers, 1970), pp. 20–21.

5. Karl Marx, *The Economic and Philosophic Manuscripts of 1844* (New York: International Publishers, 1964), p. 111.

6. *Ibid.,* p. 107.

7. *Ibid.,* pp. 109–10.

8. *Ibid.,* p. 110.

9. *Ibid.,* p. 121.

10. Robert C. Tucker, *Philosophy and Myth in Karl Marx* (Cambridge: Cambridge University Press, 1961), p. 145.

11. Marx, *Manuscripts,* p. 107.

12. *Ibid.,* p. 111.

13. *Ibid.*, p. 113.

14. *Ibid.*, p. 114.

15. Marx, *Critique of Political Economy*, p. 34.

16. Karl Marx, *Capital* I, (New York: International Publishers, 1967), p. 114.

17. Karl Marx, *Capital* I, p. 41.

18. *Ibid.*, p. 42.

19. See Roberts, *Alienation and the Soviet Economy.*

20. See, for example, Robert C. Tucker, *The Marxian Revolutionary Idea* (New York: Norton, 1969).

21. Marx, *Capital* I, p. 360.

22. *Ibid.*, p. 361.

23. *Ibid.*, p. 363.

24. *Ibid.*, p. 355.

25. *Ibid.*

26. *Ibid.*, p. 359.

27. *Ibid.*, p. 356.

28. For example, see Erich Fromm, *Marx's Concept of Man* (New York: Ungar, 1961), and Gajo Petrovic, *Marx in the Mid-Twentieth Century* (Garden City, New York: Doubleday Anchor, 1967).

29. Karl Marx, "Toward the Critique of Hegel's Philosophy of Law," in *Writings of the Young Marx on Philosophy and Society,* translated and edited by Loyd D. Easton and Kurt H. Guddat (Garden City, New York: Doubleday Anchor, 1967), pp. 252, 253.

30. Cited from Bertram Wolfe, *Three Who Made a Revolution* (New York: Dial Press, 4th rev. ed. 1964), pp. 355–56.

31. Oscar J. Hammen, "The Young Marx Reconsidered," *Journal of the History of Ideas,* Vol. XXXI, No. 1 (1970), pp. 113–14. See also his *The Red 48ers.*

32. V. I. Lenin, "A Contribution to the History of the Question of the Dictatorship" (October 20, 1920), *Collected Works,* 4th Russian edition, p. 326.

33. Cited from Robert Conquest, *The Great Terror* (London: Macmillan, 1968), p. 128.

34. Eugene Kamenka, *Marxism and Ethics* (London: Macmillan, 1969), pp. 4–5.

35. Frederick Engels, *Feuerbach, The Roots of the Socialist Philosophy* (Chicago: Charles Kerr, 1906), p. 84.

36. *Ibid.*, pp. 85–86.

37. *Ibid.*, pp. 89–90.

38. *Ibid.*, p. 89.

39. "An Interview with Kolakowski," *Encounter* (October 1971), pp. 46–47.

7: SUMMARY

1. Karl Marx, *Capital* I (New York: International Publishers, 1967), p. 75.

2. Karl Marx, *The German Ideology* (New York: International Publishers, 1947), pp. 25–26.

APPENDIX

1. Robert Clower, "The Keynesian Counterrevolution: A Theoretical Appraisal," in F. H. Hahn and F. P. R. Brechling, eds., *The Theory of Interest Rates* (London: MacMillan & Co., 1965), pp. 103–25. Axel Leijonhufvud, *On Keynesian Economics and the Economics of Keynes* (New York: Oxford University Press, 1968), pp. 49–109. Robert J. Barro and Herschel I. Grossman, "A General Disequilibrium Model of Income and Employment," *American Economic Review*, LXI, Number 1 (March 1971), pp. 82–93.

2. Paul Sweezy attempts to put Marx's analysis of crises into a Keynesian framework. See *The Theory of Capitalist Development* (New York: Monthly Review Press, 1942), pp. 133–47.

3. For a discussion of the role of Say's Law in Marx's analysis, see Bernice Shoul, "Karl Marx and Say's Law," in Joseph J. Spengler and William R. Allen, eds., *Essays in Economic Thought: Aristotle to Marshall* (Chicago: Rand McNally & Co., 1960), pp. 454–69.

4. Karl Marx, *Theories of Surplus Value*, trans. G. A. Bonner and Emile Burns (New York: International Publishers, 1952), pp. 376–78.

5. *Ibid.*, pp. 378–79.

6. *Ibid.*, p. 392.

7. This statement of Walras' Law is adopted from Oscar Lange, *Price Flexibility and Employment* (Bloomington, Indiana: The Principia Press, Inc., 1952), p. 6, note 5. See also p. 100.

8. Marx, *Theories of Surplus Value*, p. 393.

9. *Ibid.*, p. 383.

10. *Ibid.*, p. 388.

11. Karl Marx, *Capital* I (New York: International Publishers, 1967), pp. 110–13.

12. Karl Marx, *Capital* II (New York: International Publishers, 1967), p. 23.
13. Marx, *Theories of Surplus Value*, p. 385.
14. *Ibid.*, pp. 370–1.
15. *Ibid.*, p. 394.
16. Marx, *Capital* I, p. 96.
17. Clower, pp. 115–18.
18. Marx, *Theories of Surplus Value*, p. 399.
19. Barro and Grossman, pp. 84–86.
20. Marx, *Theories of Surplus Value*, p. 400–401.
21. Marx, *Capital* I, pp. 106–7.
22. Marx, *Theories of Surplus Value*, p. 412.
23. *Ibid.*, p. 410.
24. *Ibid.*, p. 408.
25. Sweezy, p. 133.

Index